CLEAR
SEEING
PLACE

CLEAR SEEING PLACE

studio visits

BRIAN RUTENBERG

permanent *green*

New York City

Published by Permanent Green, New York City

www.brianrutenbergbooks.com

Edited and Designed by Girl Friday Productions
www.girlfridayproductions.com
Editorial: Richard Koss and Dara Kaye
Interior and Cover Design: Rachel Christenson
Cover Photograph: *Spell 2*, 2015, 82 x 60 inches, oil on linen.
Courtesy of Forum Gallery, New York, NY

"There Is a Mountain" words & music by Donovan Leitch, ©1967
Donovan (Music) Ltd.
Used with permission.

Excerpt from the poem "Romantics" from *Alive Together: New and Selected Poems* by Lisel Mueller, Louisiana State University Press, lsupress.org. Reprinted with permission. All rights reserved.

ISBN-13: 978-0-9974423-0-4
eISBN: 978-0-9974423-1-1

First Edition

Printed in the United States of America

For the loves of my life, Katie, Olivia, and Christian

Contents

INTRODUCTION

First there is a mountain, then there is no mountain, then there is.

—*Donovan*

Humidity made me a painter. I was born and raised in the mind-numbing heat of coastal South Carolina. My first art lessons were wandering the banks of ancient rivers like the Waccamaw, feeling warm pluff mud squirt between my toes as I ambled from one vantage point to another, desperate to contain the view for as long as possible. Most of the 624 Saturdays of my childhood were spent near water. Long before I knew what an artist was, I'd scoop up fistfuls of marsh mud, splat them on the dock under the savage Carolina sun, and carefully arrange torn bits of colored paper across the muck, followed by another handful of mud. The frond-lipped tip of an oyster shell was an ideal tool for skimming the translucent slime to reveal jeweled flashes of color of varying intensity. I did it again and again. Everything I needed was under my feet. It took decades to recognize how much the directness and simplicity of those experiences taught me about the way a painting comes into being. Paintings aren't created; they're made. Oil paint is crushed rock mixed with liquefied fat and smeared on cloth. All of the content sits on the tip of the brush because there isn't room there for anything else. Painting enacts place.

This is not an instructional book, but a collection of thoughts, opinions, techniques, anecdotes, and personal observations spanning my days in the Lowcountry of South Carolina to my life as a full-time painter in New York City. I've also included a few trade secrets and bits of career advice because, as a magician friend once told me, if you want to keep something a secret, publish it.

Let's begin with the single most important thing you need to be a painter: a locked door. Creativity thrives on solitude. Locking your door achieves two essential goals at once—it tells the world to stay out, and it confines you to a place where self-awareness, the enemy of art, can be rinsed away; it's easier to fall in love with the sound of your voice while no one's listening. The worst thing a painter can do is edit while working. Spill everything out behind your locked door and fix it later. The time will come when you can unlock it, but for now, paint for an audience of one. Remember, you're not only the painting's maker, but also its first looker. This book will go into detail about what to expect on both sides of your door. I'll cover techniques to help you expand your vocabulary while it's locked and give you an honest idea of what to expect when you open it to the world. The art world is a business, and, like any business, it thrives on consumption, crass as that sounds. However, our *product* is antispeed. We offer a world obsessed with velocity the gift of slow seeing and slow thinking, perhaps the most sublime gift one human being can offer another. We are dreamers. Our job is to glow in the dark, and the world needs more people who glow.

Since 2010, I've been producing a series of monthly YouTube videos called "Brian Rutenberg Studio Visits" to give working artists of all levels a glimpse into my painting life. Each episode is designed to make you feel as if you've walked into my studio, pulled up a paint-crusted chair, cracked open an icy beer, and talked about work. The videos are free of charge. My payments are the emails I get every day from painters around the world sharing their stories, struggles, and victories. They remind me that I am not alone. I wrote this book to tell you the same. You are not alone. Artists have always benefited from intimate gatherings to exchange ideas and techniques and lean on one another during tough times: Thomas Eakins had the Sketch Club, Vanessa Bell had the Bloomsbury Group, Jackson Pollock had the Cedar Tavern, and we have social media. The world is getting better and better for painters because of the Internet and social media platforms like Facebook and YouTube, and we've only scratched the surface. Never has it been so easy to disseminate images to global audiences in seconds; however, as our awareness expands, there remains a hunger for the wondrous strange of the local. My videos are created in this spirit. Sometimes technology can solve the very problems it creates.

What I adore about YouTube is not watching people do mind-blowing things but knowing that anything is possible because there is always someone who can do it better. There is always room for improvement. I've watched countless hours of dimly lit painting demos that were as exciting as watching paint dry. None felt like an authentic one-on-one visit to a working artist's studio; none had the qualities I craved, including decent production value, straightforward language, humor, and, most important, joy. Why do so many painters look as if they're getting a flu shot when talking about their work? I can barely contain myself. Painting is fun. I have the best job on earth; my worst day is still better than a good day in most other jobs.

There have been many films, videos, and magazines shot in my studio, but they always look staged; I wanted something intimate and spontaneous. In early 2010, I set up recording equipment and made my first Studio Visit. It resembled a hostage video, but, after some fine-tuning with lights and angles, things improved. There are fifty-three episodes at the time of this writing, with content ranging from personal stories to ideas, materials, techniques, color mixing, and previews of new paintings, all rinsed in my love of art history. I didn't learn to speak about painting from reading books but by visiting artists' studios. A critic friend of mine agrees, noting that art criticism is different from other forms of criticism (e.g., food, film, theater, dance) because of the access accorded in a studio visit, a one-on-one encounter in the laboratory of the creator. My videos are an attempt to extend that intimacy to a broad audience through technology. This book is a companion to the videos. I've assembled the writings into six clear sections, each of which explores a primary part of my painting life. The message is simple: This is what I do and how I do it. I hope you find it useful.

LIVING

Empathy Is Gold

Art brings us back into ourselves by making us unrecognizable to ourselves; we see through someone else's eyes, which broadens our experience and gives us empathy. Painting is the most empathetic art form because the viewer stands in the exact spot that the painter did as each skin of color was stacked over time. A landscape by Paul Cézanne isn't a statement but an invocation; it whispers, "Come closer, let's twist nervous systems around one another and construct a place that wasn't there before." Will projecting our vitality onto something outside ourselves intensify our experience in the real world? You bet. I don't want a painting to educate, shock, or enlighten me; I want it to rip out my nervous system and replace it with someone else's. I want to look into what the poet Mary Oliver calls "The white fire of a great mystery." I want to drop to my knees in musky earth with Jules Breton's *The Weeders*, amble through curved space on red figure vases, and feel the stillness of Agnes Martin's grids lilt across my shoulders like a worn T-shirt in summer. Painters don't invite the viewer into a shared experience, they insist on it. Subject matter is information, and the treatment of it is what generates content. How do you see the world? Let us stare through your eyes. Show us everything, and don't leave anything out.

In his book *Hawthorne on Painting*, Charles Hawthorne wrote, "Do still life because you cannot tell a story about it—paint something that isn't anything until it is painted well. Get stuff that is supposed to be ugly, like a pie plate or an old tin basin, against a background that will bring out the beauty of the things you see. Then try to do it, trying to work for quality of color." Subject matter is the delivery system for empathy. However, we don't need to be born empathic. Art can teach it to us.

My father had empathy, always taking the side of the underdog and prompting me to consider things from other people's perspectives. Born in Brooklyn and raised in Queens, he gave up the dream of being a poet to attend Duke University and Fordham Law School like his father. After he married my movie-star-beautiful Albanian mother, they moved to the seaside resort town of Myrtle Beach, SC. Although he raised a family there, cofounded a successful law firm, and was one of the best-liked gentlemen in the state, my dad was a loner and an outsider. His poem "Bottom Lines," written in 2010, is telling:

my life turned out to be
not what i dreamt it would be
but what i let it be
which
in my case
worked

In springtime, my parents, two younger brothers, and I piled into our station wagon and drove 661 miles from our house in Myrtle Beach to New York City to see my grandparents. We stopped halfway. Virginia was sweet in April, strawberries and pale pink dogwoods under pine trees towering over redbuds, honeysuckle, grape leaves, and wild roses. My father would get out of the car and wander alone into Civil War battlefields with grown-up names like Manassas and Cedar Creek. Then he'd drop to his knees and fill glass vials with the soil that had run slimy with the blood of teenage soldiers in battle only 113 years earlier. Each bottle would be labeled and displayed on a wooden railroad tie that served as a mantel over our fireplace. To him, Virginia was a landscape ripped in half, the geographical middle between North and South, bearing the scars of both. My father was Virginia: part Yankee, part Rebel, at home in neither.

Lonely souls possess the uncanny ability to recognize it in others, so my father naturally gravitated toward misfits. While most of his colleagues played golf at country clubs, he surf fished alone, wrote poetry in his office, and drank Michelob in a suit and tie with tobacco farmers in the back of the local bait shop. He told me that you can't know someone until you've seen the world through their eyes and walked around in their shoes, a theme that runs through three of my favorite books: *To Kill a Mockingbird* by Harper Lee, *The Elephant Man and Other Reminisces* by Sir Frederick Treves, and *Death in the Grizzly Maze* by Mike Lapinski. Every morning, I try to be kind to the first stranger I meet. Small acts of kindness—holding a door, smiling with eye contact, giving up a seat on the subway—pay off in larger ways because they open up possibilities for the rest of the day. Kindness is certainly better than the opposite. Human beings make art because we desperately need an excuse to stare at one another. By glimpsing into someone else's heart, we gain a purchase on our own. Art is empathy, and it will save the world.

John Rutenberg. 1964.

Sandra Rutenberg. 1964.

It's the artists of the world, the feelers and thinkers, who will ultimately save us, who can articulate, educate, defy, insist, sing and shout the big dreams.

—*Leonard Bernstein*

Color

My first memory was blue. I was born on September 18, 1965, in Myrtle Beach, and in December of that year my parents took me by overnight train from Florence, SC (the closest station), to New York City. I remember staring at a blue nightlight in our sleeper car. My childhood was ablaze in color. As a toddler, I held my maternal grandfather's finger as he led me around his huge backyard awash in pink azaleas every March. We didn't have a lot to say (he couldn't speak English, and I couldn't speak at all), but the flowers didn't mind. Spero Michael Bogache was born in Albania and left his family behind to come through Ellis Island in 1920 with waves of immigrants seeking a better life; he had his first shave in America. How Pop-Pop loved his flowers. He guided my tiny hand across their petals and took us places words can't go. Then I'd plunge my entire head into the blossoms and open my eyes wide to burn their raucous color into my retina.

I am the product of one place with two faces. Myrtle Beach is a resort town full of amusement parks and arcades buzzing with neon signs and blinking candy-colored lights, surrounded by some of the most ravishing formal gardens on the East Coast. There is transcendent beauty in the slow-moving water of Lowcountry rivers, but artificial landscapes rinsed in nickel and neon are equally as beautiful; when my family says, "Let's get back to nature," it means book a trip to Vegas. My love affair with Las Vegas is an extension of my affection for Myrtle Beach. Both are places in which nature and artifice crash head on into each other at breakneck speed, secreting a liquid that is bright and combustible. The fullness and amplitude of my resort upbringing gave me a deep love for excess; moderation simply isn't in my vocabulary. As the South Carolina painter J. Bardin once told me, "Sometimes too much is just right."

The term "Lowcountry" originally referred to the prehistoric seacoast, or Sandhills, of South Carolina, which spanned the width of the state from Aiken to Chesterfield counties. The Upcountry was everything above the Sandhills. Today, Lowcountry refers to coastal regions, from Georgetown to Beaufort, including sea islands like St. Helena, Edisto, Fripp, Kiawah, and Port Royal. The richness of place permeates the South Carolina Lowcountry and is woven inextricably into her history, folklore, and commerce. The Romantic painter Washington Allston was born in Georgetown, SC, forty minutes south of where I was raised. He wrote of how he "delighted in being terrified by the tales of witches and hags," referring to the same tangled woods I explored as a kid. My college roommate was born and raised in McClellanville, a small shrimping village fifty minutes north of Charleston. One summer, he led me deep into the woods to visit his relatives in a nearby Gullah community, descendants of slaves who worked on the rice plantations of South Carolina and Georgia. We drove down a dirt road to a dead end and then walked beside a river flowing black as typewriter ink; decaying tree trunks peeking from waterlogged shadows like gargoyles made the familiar appear alien. Cobalt-blue bottles tinkled in branches overhead, put there to ward off wooly boogers (hairy monsters that live deep in the Southern woods) who, attracted to the light refracting through the glass, became trapped and vaporized in the morning sun. Blue is thought to repel evil spirits, which is why porch ceilings down south are often painted the color of sky. I still think of those bottles when I use bright blue.

I use bright colors because they're available. Twentieth-century hues like pthalo green, quinacridone magenta, and Hansa yellow have high tinting strength and can be quite intense. However, the key to using bright colors effectively is knowing how to use dull ones. Adding bright color is like turning a radio up a little at a time; you don't realize how loud it is until you turn it down. Dull colors are like turning the radio down. I spent decades practicing with tertiaries, even studying the gray muck in the bottom of my paint thinner bucket because it feels like the gooey pluff mud that I marinated in for the first eighteen years of my life. Mud always fascinated me, and I whipped up mud pies better than any kid in school, but I never got the memo that you couldn't eat them. Oil paint is just organized dirt, and I've tasted that too.

The Lowcountry wore softer palettes. My love affair with the color of oysters began at an early age. At low tide, their shells, delicate as pastry, cupped shallow puddles of salt water and pale mud. I'd lie on my stomach examining their color, just a breath of itself, and imagine swimming in their palm-sized oceans. Decades later, I realized this wasn't the daydreaming of a child, but the mechanics of how a painter sees the world. Scale and logic evaporate, replaced by a new reality that is bright and capricious. There isn't a color more beautiful than that of an oyster shell. Well, maybe that of a glazed Krispy Kreme doughnut.

My list of great colorists probably overlaps with yours (Fra Angelico, Pontormo, Henri Matisse, Pierre Bonnard, Hans Hofmann, and Josef Albers), so I won't focus on a stupid top-ten list. However, I learn just as much from lesser-known artists like Samuel Peploe, F.H. Varley, Karl Benjamin, Spencer Gore, Goodridge Roberts, Joseph Solman, Sonia Delaunay, and Bob Thompson. I never begin with a preconceived color plan but mix and juxtapose unexpected combinations right on the canvas until a family, usually three colors, starts to suggest a mood, much like Edwin Dickinson's "color spots," in which he would apply one tone next to another, gradually building color space. Through trial and error, I discovered certain color pairings that I stick with, such as purple/green, brown/blue, teal/orange, and red/gray. I keep several palettes going simultaneously and mix large amounts of one color in a range of tones on each palette. I also have one palette with small blobs of color arranged in the order of the spectrum. Plastic Chinese food containers are ideal for mixing.

Although I painted in acrylics early in my career, I am an oil painter. Oil colors are transparent, semitransparent, or opaque. Transparents such as alizarin crimson or pthalo green are fat (high oil content), while opaques like cadmium red or cerulean blue are lean (low oil content). Titanium white is opaque and is the whitest white, while zinc white is semitransparent and good for glazing. Black is a highly versatile color, and I am always suspicious of teachers who advise against using it. Diego Velázquez used black—end of discussion. I prefer ivory black (semitransparent) and mars black (opaque), both of which have warm tints perfect for dirtying other colors. Mars black mixed with alizarin crimson makes a black cherry color and, when mixed with lemon yellow, produces a gorgeous dull green.

At first glance my paintings appear to have every color imaginable. The human eye can detect more than seven million variations, but the more you look you will see that they operate chromatically within a small orbit of a few carefully chosen hues. It's never about individual colors but how they vibrate together: purple appears more intense when placed near yellow or green. Vincent van Gogh kept a red Chinese lacquered box on his worktable in which he stored balls of colored yarn that were woven in multiple combinations to help him visualize what brushstrokes might look like on a canvas. His pal Émile Bernard noted their "unexpected interlacing tonalities" in which colors in combination produced greater effect than individually. A good place to experiment with color juxtapositions is in the house paint section of your local hardware store. Try moving the little color sample swatches around in various combinations—just don't get caught.

The key to color is to try everything without scrutiny. Just play. You can't think color; you have to see it. I've never taken a color theory class in my life but rely on direct observation and practice. Color is communication. It can stir our deepest emotions, create a sense of spaciousness, and momentarily distract us from the unstoppable advance of time with sheer visual delight. However, you don't learn color from books; you have to monkey around with it on your palette, put a blob next to another blob, and see how they look together. Work across the image rather than on top of it. In other words, don't labor over parts, but work the whole field; if you put a dab of cobalt blue in one spot, move it to the opposite side swiftly, without analysis. Do, then think.

The director Arthur Penn said that every day on set he made one decision that changed the entire film. He just didn't know which one. By doing first and thinking second, I have assembled an unusual and personal pal-ette. Some combinations work and others fail, but all it takes is one good decision and the entire painting hums. The secret is to pay attention.

Paying Attention

Every spring during childhood, my mother placed a crystal bowl of water on my bedside table in which floated three pink camellia blossoms cut from a bush in our front yard. At night, I'd lie on my pillow, watching them slowly spin and bump into each other until my eyelids betrayed me. They would still be spinning when I awoke. Looking is gathering information, but seeing is contemplation. My mother was teaching me how to see. She created the conditions for an experience that had no intrinsic meaning whatsoever, yet it filled me with a rage to live.

There is too much focus on meaning in contemporary art; people want to know what it means. They need to understand. This desire to know is logical if you're reading a pill bottle, but painting is seldom logical. Seeing a painting takes patience and the willingness to perceive differently. It restacks our priorities in unexpected ways and entices us to notice that which we overlooked. When a painter does their job well, the richness of content supplants the requirement for meaning. Van Gogh painted a pair of old shoes on a table, but we don't need to know what he meant to access acres of rich content because of *how* he painted them. Everything we need is compressed into each ropey brushstroke. All that's required is our full presence.

I love the fact that a painting is an object made solely to be seen, enabling us to unbuckle from linear thought and drift. However, drifting implies moving away from something. What is my something? If you had asked me to define my work as either abstraction or representation thirty years ago, I'd have barked out the former. Now I'm not so sure. I am not an *abstract* artist. What does that even mean? I am a landscape painter who constructs images by abstracting from the visible world. Abstraction is a process, not a style. Saying you're painting abstracts is like saying you're eating cooking: it doesn't mean anything. To abstract means to *remove*, which implies it must be removed from something. I no longer believe that a painting can be about paint. Philip Guston was right: "Painting is impure." He goes on, "We are image-makers and image-ridden." What get promoted as *abstracts* in many galleries are actually representational paintings of abstraction, pushing paint around in a manner that looks like art, usually someone else's. What are you abstracting from? My paintings must extend from real things; otherwise they look too much like art. It's fashionable to claim that your work is open to interpretation or that it can be about whatever the viewer wants, but that's marketing horseshit. What are you communicating? Sure, painting realistic water droplets on a chicken is impressive, but that's not art. Some painters have a voice and lousy technique, while others have astounding facility but no soul; they're just taking victory laps. Those who possess both have molten lava. Be yourself—the rest is just constant practice.

When I Knew

On my sixth birthday, my parents drove me one hundred miles south to Charleston to have my portrait done by Alicia Rhett, a well-known pastel artist who did some acting on the side; she played opposite Olivia de Havilland as Melanie Wilkes's sister India in a little film called *Gone with the Wind*. For several consecutive Saturdays, I sat on a licorice-black stool in the parlor of her antebellum carriage house, which smelled of furniture polish and soup. The sound of pastel on cream Fabriano Tiziano paper lulled me into a trance. I paid attention and asked questions. On the right side of her easel was an antique table bearing the tools of work: stumps in porcelain teacups, pale chamoise skins, blending tortillions, and battalions of pastels lined up as neatly as a diamondback's markings. What kind of job was this? I wondered. My father sat in a room full of law books; his father sat in the same room in a different zip code. What is an artist's job? For the first time, I realized there was a subspecies of human beings who roamed the earth able to see that which was hidden in plain sight. I sensed the comforting murmur of family—not that of my parents and brothers, but a subtler music. Being an artist is familial.

I watched as she transformed a few crumbs of cobalt blue into my right eye, as blue as the real thing, even more so. Instinctively, I reached out my finger and smeared the iris that had taken days to craft. She must have wanted to hit me with a polo mallet, but I'll never forget what she said:

"You're going to be an artist, Brian. I'm certain of it."

Pastel portrait by Alicia Rhett. 1971.

The best picture makes us say, I am a painter also.

—*Ralph Waldo Emerson*

. . . *And It's Deep, Too*

Myrtle Beach offered little exposure to the fine arts. The art section at Booksmith, our only bookstore, offered two choices: a book on garden gnomes and a collection of perforated stencils for shaving designs into your pubic hair called *Naughty Notions*. I could only afford one.

With my new collection of stencils, I retired to the privacy of our bathroom and carved a yin-yang into my pale fifteen-year-old bush with my father's Gillette razor; it looked as if I'd been mauled by a puma. Still hungry (and itchy), I discovered the art history section in the public library and devoured it shelf by shelf. My favorite book was a full-color collection of the sea battle paintings of Édouard Manet. Much of what I know about suggesting volume and space in painting comes from that book. Despite filling dozens of watercolor pads with weak imitations, I still couldn't understand how Manet got such elastic space on a flat, lifeless surface. The answer wasn't in my brain, but under it. I noticed how the corners of my pillow bulged under the weight of my head when I lay down to go to sleep. The shapes changed as my weight shifted.

After school the following day, I walked to a nearby creek and gathered rocks that corresponded to the sizes and colors of the ships in Manet's paintings. Then, I carefully arranged them on a turquoise-colored pillow in the same orientation. Heavier rocks sunk lower; smaller stones sat higher. The deeper the depression in one spot, the more inflated the bulge in another. Weight and counterweight are integral components in constructing paintings; each stroke displaces another, and the entire image changes. My mother bought every turquoise pillow in town as I churned out working studies of the entire book. While my friends were outside playing basketball, I was in my room playing with rocks and pillows. That's how someone stays a virgin until twenty-two.

Tired of buying pillows and razors, my mother asked the English teacher, who also painted, if he would give me some watercolor lessons after school. His name was Tom. Once a week, my brother John, a girl named Melissa, who had blonde pigtails, and I appeared at the classroom with our watercolor pads. Tom would close the door, put on a Richard Pryor album, and we'd paint. I took devilish pleasure in the fact that there was one kind of school from eight to two thirty, but at three o'clock, a different kind of school began. The timing, irreverence, and freedom in those comedy albums taught me to relax, breathe, and be myself while I worked. They also taught me how to use repetition as a compositional device, just as a comedian structures a joke in threes: two to establish a pattern and one to break it. Penn Jillette and Paul Provenza's terrific 2005 film *The Aristocrats* features over one hundred comedians telling the same joke to explore the richness and breadth of artists working within formal limitations; George Carlin and Miles Davis do essentially the same thing, just in different media. Each riffs within rules. They begin and end alone and exposed, attempting to create a world that is spacious and untenable, dying a little with each performance. I still play Richard Pryor in my studio late at night to further my education.

If you don't live it, it won't come out of the horn.
—*Charlie Parker*

Animal

I played drums seriously throughout high school and was very good. In addition to my rock bands Impulse and XXX, which performed in front of thousands of people in South Carolina, North Carolina, and Georgia, I had a jazz trio and played percussion in a Renaissance music consort called the Charleston Pro Musica; I still have my mustard-colored tunic and wear it when I want to see my kids vomit. I never intended to make a living as an artist. My plan was to make money from music to support painting, which is like selling poems to support a juggling career. Like most plans, it didn't work.

My undergraduate studies began in 1983 at the College of Charleston in Charleston, SC. Within days of my arrival, I immersed myself in its excellent School of the Arts. My first painting class was William Halsey's last. Born in 1915, Halsey is considered the father of abstract painting in South Carolina. His fully dimensional use of color was an early influence on my work, as were the poetic images of Corrie McCallum, his wife. Corrie and I also shared a love of chamber music and would eat grilled cheese sandwiches while listening to Bartók string quartets in her Archdale Street studio. My work ethic impressed the faculty, and soon I was given not one but two private studios on opposite ends of the fine arts department, one for painting and one for my massive drum kit. I also scored a master key to every room in the building, which no one knew about, until now. Whenever I was struggling with a new painting, I would drag it from my studio to my drum room and play as I looked at the painting. Somehow, having all four of my limbs moving in syncopation while looking at a static image intensified my understanding of the inanimate nature of oil paint, reminding me that vitality is not rendered by the artist, but projected by the viewer. Paint is passive; looking is active.

Although I had a dormitory with roommates on campus, I secretly lived in the fine arts building, where I'd paint into the early morning and sleep on a dirty orange bench carried up from the lobby each night. I returned it before sunrise. On more than one occasion, faculty members—and even visiting prospective students and their parents—unlocked my studio door to find me splayed out in my underwear, snoring. They never said a word.

Each week, in the middle of the night, I installed massive multipaneled paintings that sprawled across the floor, up the wall, and onto the ceiling; people couldn't move through the public spaces without navigating through my painted environments. No one gave me permission; I just did stuff. That kind of unchecked liberty empowered me to explore other disciplines: I built a stage set for the Robert Ivey Ballet, worked in the costume shop, made sculpture in the foundry, cataloged slides in the art history library, and installed shows in the college's art gallery.

Every spring the Halsey Gallery (now the Halsey Institute of Contemporary Art) sponsored a "Young Contemporaries" exhibition in which an outside curator was invited to select the strongest students for a polished, one-month-long show. Two of my paintings were included in 1985. Until then I had never seen my work displayed on a clean, well-lit wall, because I destroyed everything after making it. Not being precious allowed me to move swiftly through mistakes and eliminate what didn't interest me. I sat by the gallery door all night long eating Hardee's cinnamon buns washed down with burnt coffee so I'd be the first one to install my work. From that show, I was handpicked by David L. Shirey, chair of the Master of Fine Arts Program at the School of Visual Arts in New York City, to enter its two-year MFA program. I was moving to New York.

I can't say enough about the importance of a faculty that catapults students into new experiences and allows them the permission to make mistakes along the way. The School of the Arts at the College of Charleston was my home and the entire building was my working space. There were complaints that I was too aggressive, but no action was taken. Someone had my back.

Performing with the Charleston Pro Musica. 1987.

With my high school rock band Impulse.
I made the fake gong out of cardboard and paint. 1983.

Landing in NYC

In May 1987, I graduated from the College of Charleston and, three weeks later, moved to New York City to attend the Master of Fine Arts Program at the School of Visual Arts. I was twenty-one years old and had never lived in a big city. To me, crack was something you did to an egg, rush hour was getting to the beach by high tide to go fishing, and a power lunch was grilled cheese on the hood of a car. I took a yellow taxi to 133 W. Twenty-First Street with two large black Samsonite suitcases, one full of brushes and the other my clothes, which included an emergency envelope containing $500 cash and a one-way plane ticket back to Myrtle Beach on Piedmont Airlines in case things didn't work out. Those suitcases have followed me to every studio since and serve a symbolic as well as practical purpose. Because of my height, my worktable needs to be higher than the standard tables found in office supply stores. Laying the suitcases on their sides and resting the table legs on top brings my eight-foot-long work surface to an ideal waist level. The present is supported by the past, literally. One of those suitcases remains unopened. The emergency envelope and plane ticket within are unused. Piedmont doesn't even exist anymore. I guess things worked out.

My first New York residence was the Sloane House YMCA on Thirty-Fourth Street and Ninth Avenue, near Madison Square Garden. Now luxury condominiums, "Slime House" in the late 1980s was a cheap, dimly lit lodging residence teeming with hookers and the semihomeless. My tenth-floor "suite" was so small that I could lie in bed and open the door with my toes. The fluorescent-lit communal men's bathroom featured yellow shower curtains with dick-sized holes cut at waist level, hair-clogged sinks, and shelves littered with bottles of Gas-X and lube; one morning, I saw a dead body under a white sheet on a gurney being rolled out of the kitchen, heads of lettuce keeping the sheet from blowing off in the wind; pour one out for the poor bastards who ordered salad that night. I was never happier.

Every morning, I'd grab a black coffee at the corner deli and walk thirteen blocks downtown to my Twenty-First Street studio. For the next two years, I never deviated from that routine, not even once. Something uncanny happens when you repeat the same behavior thousands of times: the familiar becomes unrecognizable. I noticed perfectly bound bundles of cardboard that migrated from basements up to the curb for sanitation pickup in the predawn darkness. Like soft caramels stamped with Chinese logos in dark green ink, those cubes enticed me so much that I dragged them into my studio and created multi-paneled cardboard paintings on which I drew with electrical tape, wire, polyurethane, charcoal, and oil paint. They were organic and open-ended environments that swelled into every part of the room, incorporating the radiator, windows, and fire escape. At the suggestion of the sculptor Ursula von Rydingsvard, I decided to limit my palette to mars black and buff white; all other color had to come from found materials. Cardboard is the color of cubism. I had been studying the analytic cubist paintings of Georges Braque and noted how their limited palette drew attention to line and structure.

My studio brimmed with so many cardboard pieces that I would leave them on the steps of random brownstones in Chelsea on my walk back to the dorm late each night. The following morning, I'd spot them on the curb with the morning trash; however, more than once, I saw them through the window hanging on a wall. Either way, it didn't matter, because my goal was to make something from the street and return it there. My teachers were delighted because they had an entirely new body of work to talk about every two weeks, after which I would destroy everything and start over. Nothing was precious. I was making work, not art.

The School of Visual Arts, or SVA, was fabulous. David Shirey and his administrator, Kathy Schnapper, were kind to me. They still are. The program was intellectually stimulating, and I was challenged to question and reinvent myself. There was decent studio space, twenty-four-hour access, and no limits. In addition, the school operated its own art gallery on Prince Street in SoHo, which was the center of the New York art world in those days. I was fortunate to have been included in several faculty-curated group exhibitions, which gave students hands-on experience in how to construct a gallery show from concept to transportation, installation, promotion, and opening reception. I even made sales and gained some useful contacts. At SVA, I studied closely with well-known artists and critics like Darby Bannard, Robert Mangold, Judy Pfaff, Ursula von Rydingsvard, Jackie Winsor, Joe Zucker, Loren Madsen, Clement Greenberg, and Vito Acconci. However, one teacher towered over the others like the Empire State Building. His name was Gregory Amenoff.

*Studio shot. 2016. The two black suitcases I used to move
to New York now support my painting table.*

Early hallway show. School of Visual Arts, New York City.
1987.

After Graduate School

After graduating from SVA with a master's degree in 1989, I moved into a dark three-hundred-square-foot ground-floor studio apartment in Jackson Heights, Queens, for $365 a month, which I could barely afford. Queens is the most boring of the five boroughs, and boredom is jet fuel for creativity. I took long evening walks down Northern Boulevard, read poetry in the back of Jackson Diner, and made small paintings in my room living on Peanut Butter Cap'n Crunch and sweet iced tea. To earn money, I did art handling, worked as a studio assistant, and helped out in two art galleries. My expenses were low enough to afford the maximum amount of time in the apartment. On one side of my room was a single bed with a small television and my complete *Star Trek* video collection. On the other was a blue tarp that covered the beige carpet and most of the wall as protection from flying paint. In the middle of the tarp was an old floor-tom from my drum kit, which doubled as an easel on which to lean paintings, and I mixed colors directly on the drumhead. Except for a couple of group shows in the South, I stayed alone in my room and worked.

By 1992, I had a decent body of small paintings and, at the suggestion of Gregory Amenoff, applied for a grant from the Marie Walsh Sharpe Art Foundation, which awards twenty-eight free studios to working artists for a year. I got one. My corner studio on Greenwich and Vestry Streets in TriBeCa faced the original World Trade Center Towers seven blocks downtown. I loved those towers and would eat turkey sandwiches on the roof at night while gazing up at their immensity. For the first time, my life was getting interesting, I thought. With hard work, it might even become fascinating.

Me in my tiny Queens apartment and studio. 1989.

I love New York, even though it isn't mine, the way something has to be, a tree or a street or a house, something, anyway, that belongs to me because I belong to it.

—*Truman Capote*

Renting Studio Space

After a productive year in the studio program, it was time to vacate, so three fellow "Sharpies" and I pooled our money and rented a huge empty space on the fifth floor of the same building, 443 Greenwich Street. We did the demo and build-out ourselves, dividing a raw space into five spacious private studios, which we named "Five on Five": my studiomates and I would remain there for sixteen years until someone planted a $400 million maple tree in front of the lobby. Allegedly, an investor bought the entire building for $200 million with plans to sink another $200 million into creating a boutique hotel and condominium complex. That fucking tree meant that we should look for other forests. Rents were tripled, and we were forced out.

No matter—artists are survivors, always a step ahead of everyone else. We move on to other neighborhoods, make them hip, and the cycle repeats. My studiomates and I found bigger, better digs in the Flatiron District. We rented the entire sixth floor of a new building, took on two extra tenants to defray costs, and renamed ourselves "Six on Six." New York is wicked expensive. Having studiomates is the only way to find affordable workspace.

Working in Galleries

Contrary to claims by other great cities, New York City is still the capital of the art world. A handful of blue-chip galleries create art stars and determine values, big auction houses brand them, and critics write about them. Although the contemporary art world likes to think of itself as open-minded and inclusive, it is tribal and conservative. As we all learned in high school, when there are insiders, there are outsiders.

From 1987 to 1995, I worked at Cavin-Morris Gallery, which is owned by Shari Cavin and Randall Morris, pioneers in the field of self-taught and folk art. It was a joyful space, reverberating with music, lively conversation, and the spicy bouquet of Jamaican takeout. Regulars included Jonathan Demme, Tony Fitzpatrick, Ellen Page Wilson, Bert Hemphill, David Byrne, Geoffrey Holder, Eric Bogosian, and the late playwright Lanford Wilson, who had just finished *Burn This* when we met. Lanford was an avid art collector and took a special interest in me because I had just moved to New

York City from the South. We would talk about our respective Lowcountry and Ozark cultures (he was born and raised in Lebanon, Missouri) and how an artist can grow a rich lexicon of language and imagery over a lifetime by continually tilling the loam of a specific region. We also discussed religion. He was raised Baptist and I a Methodist. Then there was cheese. Lanford rhapsodized on the splendors of fine aged cheddar from the heartland with adjectives like "sulfuric" and "barnyardy."

Such strong personalities kept things fresh and unpredictable in the front room. However, my education took place in the back with the storage racks. I couldn't imagine a better classroom for a young painter, because it immersed me in the visions of artists who made work utterly devoid of cynicism. Self-taught artists don't need the art world or its approval; they don't even need art supplies. A ballpoint pen was a scalpel in the hand of Chelo Amezcua, and a mealy paste of soot and saliva on shirt board was all James Castle required to chart intimate and complex systems. Each created personal universes that would have arisen regardless of whether the art world was looking. Theirs is not art about art, but a way of fitting into this world by inventing another. I kept my pie hole shut and my eyes open.

An art school education is like an air bag. A trained artist can employ fluid drawing technique and deft color handling to create competent sophisticated paintings, but sometimes too much skill insulates the artist from the viewer. That insulation is missing in self-taught art. I developed a deep love for, and bought works by, Jon Serl, James Castle, George Liautaud, William Edmondson, Joseph Yoakum, Kevin Sampson, Gregory Van Maanen, and Bessie Harvey, paying off paintings in installments with a small percentage of each paycheck.

More than a job, that experience stamped my passport for entrance into the vast country of the New York art world by teaching me to avoid trends and stay grounded amid the cutthroat competitiveness of the market. Most of all, it taught me that if there is no inside, there is no outside, only good and bad painting. I'm a mainstream artist, but my heart beats with the mavericks.

Jon Serl and me. 1992.

I paint so I can fuck a little longer.

—*Jon Serl*

New York Debut

A solo show in New York City is an honor and a big deal. Mine was in 1993 in that same gallery. One of Cavin-Morris's prominent clients, Peter Du Bois, had seen my paintings in a local group show and started buying everything I made. Although I already had an impressive résumé, my work hadn't gained much traction in the Northeast, so the timing was ideal. Without my knowledge, Peter invited Randall and Shari to his cavernous TriBeCa loft for a viewing. They liked what they saw and asked for a studio visit. Fortunately, I had just completed a new body of work during my tenure at the Marie Walsh Sharpe Foundation that would eventually become my River Paintings. I had also joined the Stephen Wirtz Gallery in San Francisco on Greg Amenoff's recommendation, so the decision was made to mount solo exhibitions on both coasts.

In September 1993, "River Paintings" opened in New York and San Francisco with a handsome catalog written by critic/artist Stephen Westfall; that publication occasionally appears on eBay. Both shows were well attended, got a great review in *Art in America*, and sold out. I asked for half of my earnings in cash because I wanted to have a pillowcase full of money to go with my pillowcase of rejection letters from galleries, a matching set. My mother often sent me care packages with clean bed linens; I painted on cardboard because I couldn't afford canvas but I slept on six-hundred-thread-count Egyptian cotton sheets. Although it was terrific that the paintings sold, it was to whom that was notable: small- and medium-sized art museums; the South Carolina Arts Commission; the Federal Reserve Bank; European, Middle Eastern, and Asian collectors; and even other respected New York art dealers like Allan Stone and Spencer Throckmorton. When a reporter asked me how it felt to have such a successful debut in New York City, I said it felt wonderful, but I say the same thing about every show no matter where it is. Whether the work sells or not, an exhibition anywhere is a privilege, not a right. Those rejection letters never let me forget how fortunate I am. Besides, a drummer can always find a job, right?

When asked to list my career highlights, I don't have any. Everything is a highlight. Amateurs have triumphs; I just show up every day and make stuff. All it takes is one person to change everything. The trick is to recognize them. The circus performer Karl Wallenda said, "Life is the wire. The rest is just waiting." That spring a twenty-one-year-old NYU art history major with chocolate eyes and a pale blue sundress walked into the gallery. My wire was about to happen.

Selecting work for my NYC gallery debut.
Cavin-Morris Gallery. 1992.

To feel. To trust the feeling. I long for that.

—*Ingmar Bergman*

Katie

In 1993, on the recommendation of the art historian Ed Sullivan, twenty-one-year-old Kathryn Peck was hired by Cavin-Morris Gallery as a part-time assistant. I had recently joined their stable of artists but worked there two days a week to supplement my income. She was the most beautiful woman I'd ever seen. She still is. On our breaks we'd talk about Rainer Maria Rilke and Sandro Botticelli over carrot muffins with cream cheese frosting washed down with iced coffee from Dean & Deluca. I took fake sips to stretch my time with her as long as possible. Sometimes I'd walk her home. Katie lived in the heart of Greenwich Village on Bleecker and MacDougal, and my apartment was at 23 Grove Street and Bedford. Just as we were becoming good friends, I was awarded a studio grant and quit the gallery to paint full-time. Katie subsequently left to start premed at NYU. Although we fell out of touch, she never left my mind. After two failed relationships,

I was determined to find her again. She was looking for me too.

Three years later, Katie returned to the gallery hoping to find me and reconnect. She signed the guest book. By chance, I came in the following day and noticed her signature, the last one on that page. Had one more visitor scrawled his or her name, it would have started a new page, and my life would be very different. I ran back to my apartment and composed a long handwritten letter, which ended with my phone number. After a three-hour call, we agreed to meet at my pal Kevin Sampson's opening and after-party; my friends said they could see electrical sparks between us at dinner. Early the next morning, as the city slept, I sat in a tiny Greenwich Village bedroom and wrote my wedding toast.

The reason I am telling you all of this is that the secret to my success as an artist was marrying the right person. The love and stability of a good marriage to a self-reliant spouse can knock the legs out from under any problem the world can fling at your windshield. It was the most important decision of my life, and I nailed it. Now I could get to work.

Katie and me. 2014.

As azure is to the eagle, as to the ship the sea.
As the deer is to the wildwood, so you are home
to me.

—Archibald Rutledge

Being a Father
and a Painter

I can't remember a time when I didn't want to be a daddy. Katie and I have two beautiful children, but balancing a career and family is not easy; it's agony to leave the studio when a painting sucks and reset into domestic life, homework, dinnertime, baths, and the many phases of bedtime. After my kids are tucked in, I take a scalding hot shower to Frank Sinatra and dry off under the hair dryer on the hottest setting. Then, I drink a glass of ice water and collapse into bed. As I drift to sleep, my mind ponders other types of work, critical jobs such as police officer, doctor, soldier, firefighter, and teacher. I try to imagine losing a bleeding patient in the operating room or shouldering eighty pounds of equipment up a flight of stairs in thousand-degree heat, and I remember that an artist has the best job on earth.

Every morning, I ride the subway with my fellow New Yorkers going to their respective jobs. They wear gray business suits or silk dresses; others don uniforms decorated with logos such as UPS or FedEx. I dress like a middle-aged fat guy going to a kegger. Most people carry a briefcase or backpack. This morning I had a rubber hose and a DVD boxed set of *Green Acres*. My job is weird, but the thought of not doing it is weirder. I know how fortunate I am. When a doctor has a bad day, someone dies; a lousy day for a painter is the wrong tone of pink. But our job is critical in other ways. There is no culture unless we show up for work. Artists aren't team players; we're narcissistic, easily offended, often medicated, and blue. (I realize I've just described Cookie Monster.) We're dreamers, and there is no civilization without dreamers. We don't do it for the attention and certainly not for the money. We do it for the pure love of the thing. Kenneth Clark wrote, "Facts become art through love." A painter must fall madly in love with absolutely everything. The instant that work becomes labor, you're dead.

Having children made me a better artist because I feel a love that I didn't think possible, as if a new organ sprouted in my chest. Fatherhood also meant that I'd worry every minute for the rest of my life. The first couple of years are just suicide watch, keeping fingers out of outlets and little feet away from stairs, but when a child's personality emerges, it is wondrous and funny beyond words.

When my daughter asked if I was the tooth fairy, I said, "Yes, honey, I am the fairy."

She thought for a moment. "You fly all over the world and collect the children's teeth?"

My heart filled with joy because we saw the same thing from two different vantage points. To an adult, a child's toy is trivial. However, the world that child creates around it is rich and spacious. I don't know about you, but my childhood was spent in blissful boredom, fishing in lakes and wandering along creek beds with nothing to do; a single day seemed to last forever. There were no plans, only happenings. Ask any kid to describe their day, and they'll say, "This happened. Then this happened. Then that happened." Painting restores the spaciousness of childhood and reminds us of things we knew but forgot, because art is carefully orchestrated wandering. If you're in a hurry, you'll miss everything. To be a painter, you must have more patience than anyone else in the room and know how to disappear in plain view. Becoming a father taught me both. Plus, how seriously can you take yourself while wiping someone's boogers on a tree?

Dear to me is sleep: still more, being made of
stone,
While pain and guilt still linger here below,
Blindness and numbness—these please me
alone;
Then do not wake me, keep your voices low.
                    —*Michelangelo Buonarroti*

Freedom

My father died of stage IV lung cancer on September 17, 2012, the day before my forty-seventh birthday. Two days later, I opened a solo exhibition at Jerald Melberg Gallery in Charlotte, NC. His last words to me were, "Don't miss your opening." I attended my reception in a black suit, did a slide talk the next morning, got into a van with a thermos of black coffee, and returned to Myrtle Beach for the funeral wearing the same suit, all within thirty-six hours. You can watch that slide talk on Vimeo by typing "Jerald Melberg, Brian Rutenberg Coffee & Conversation 2012." You'll see me tear up when I mention him.

When my father was the age I am now (fifty), he was surf fishing alone on a silvery Carolina Sunday and hooked a hundred-dollar bill. After untangling the soggy note from strands of seaweed, he drove his blue station wagon to Western Sizzler and ordered the biggest steak on the menu, medium rare. Then he drove back to the beach, crouched on the hard sand, and ate the meat with his bare hands.

Following his death, after my next show opened in New York City, I took a hundred-dollar bill from the ATM, walked to Old Homestead Steakhouse on Ninth Avenue and Fourteenth Street, and ordered the biggest rib eye on the menu, medium rare. Then, I sat on a stoop in the Village and ate the meat with my hands. It tasted like freedom.

WANDERING

Why Landscape?

To experience transcendence, you must know your origins. Where do you come from? What place stacked your bones into the shape of you? I live in the most cosmopolitan city on earth, yet I look more like an overweight Greek waiter than a "dazzling urbanite," to borrow a line from *Blazing Saddles*. My wife, Katie, and I wear black to fancy receptions, but I'm never more than one burp away from the beach bum that I really am, preferring flip-flops, shorts, and a T-shirt, even on chilly days. I don't take myself very seriously, but I do know on which side my bread is buttered; I know where I come from. The most soulful paintings are tethered to one idea, one place, a single heat source, and no place burns hotter than the American South.

Because it remained somewhat separate from the Western expansion of the United States in the nineteenth century, the South was perceived as complex, isolated, and exotic, an ideal breeding ground for eccentrics, storytellers, songwriters, and artists. You know as well as I that there isn't one Southern land-scape any more than there is a single Southern identity, yet all of us lucky enough to have been born there wear the same tattoo of geography across our sunburnt shoulders. I live in New York City, but I'm tied to the shape of the Carolina coast, whose tangled woods and oppressive heat don't represent progress over nature but defeat at its hands. I grew up in landscapes so hauntingly beautiful that it was unbearable. As a kid, I believed that I could see the languid air that stuck to my eyelids and hung like curtains at dusk. The South spawns many writers and artists because it's so damn hot, and heat makes people crazy. Some artists seek inspiration in her languorous scenery, while others sur-render to humidity's curfew and allow their eyes to be torched by untamed light. That's the difference between a landscape painter and a *Southern* landscape painter; a Southern landscape painter extracts poetry from capit-ulation. An artist is born the moment he or she gives up. If you're making art, you're trying too hard. Stop it. The best paintings look like work, not art. I gave up trying long ago and what was left over, that sleep-deprived, desperate version of myself, was my spark. I've built a successful career fanning that spark.

Southern children are taught to drink in the won-drous details of the local landscape: a flower isn't just a flower but a blue water hyssop or Southern marsh canna, birds are black-bellied whistling ducks or red-footed boobies, and barbecue sauce is light tomato, heavy tomato, mustard, or vinegar. Poetry lives in details, and the artist's job is to amplify them. My connection to the landscape of South Carolina has nothing to do with nostalgia; it's much broader than memory. It's my clear seeing place. A career has many moving parts, but there must be a cable that runs from your soft tissue directly to your clear-seeing place.

Every artist needs such a place, for this is where your muse resides. Mine is an old man named Homiah. He has gray sideburns and wears a shabby brown trench coat and a Gatsby cap. Homiah has been my muse for as long as I can remember. The reason that I work all day, every day, is so that Homiah will know when and where to find me; I lock my door, start messing around, and pretty soon he appears, all soft-mouthed and weightless. His only prerequisite is solitude.

As a kid, I found solitude in cardboard boxes. I'd find a rectangular box slightly bigger than my body, drag it into the woods, cram it into the bushes, and crawl inside. I wasn't escaping anything so much as seeking containment amid wildness. Remoteness entices me. As a teenager I'd take our eight-foot john-boat down the Waccamaw River into hidden coves, where I'd smear a marmalade of cold river mud on my face and bare chest. Then, I'd lie on the floor of the boat and drift with the current. The fecund smell of river water clears my mind, and I need it on a regular basis.

If I can't travel to a remote location, then I summon it in my imagination. Urban life has taught me by necessity how to withdraw into myself on command as an electric eel generates voltage. Manhattan can be whatever you need: busy or lonely, rapid or glacially slow. I have the best family ever and plenty of friends, but I love to be alone and feel fortunate to have a career that demands solitude.

Every year, I take at least one trip alone in which I can drive and listen to the radio. These trips are not always to remote locations. They sometimes dovetail with other interests: magic conventions, *Star Trek* conventions, Graceland, casinos, and once even a celebration of the 1980s television show *Dallas* (I'm a big fan), which included a barbecue dinner on Southfork Ranch hosted by the original cast. Avid enthusiasm for interests other than painting is an integral part of my practice because through them I get to know myself better.

While driving alone through the stark Nevada desert, I heard a beautiful poem by Lisel Mueller called "Romantics" on NPR's *Writer's Almanac*. The poem contemplates the close friendship between Johannes Brahms and Clara Schumann. It closes with words that have stayed with me ever since: "Each time I hear the Intermezzi, sad and lavish in their tenderness, I imagine the two of them sitting in a garden among late-blooming roses and dark cascades of leaves, letting the landscape speak for them, leaving us nothing to overhear."

The words "leaving us nothing to overhear" articulate something I have felt for a very long time. Art isn't the reliving of an experience, but the total possessing of it. Artists have long invented multisensory ways of possessing the landscape around them: witness the St Ives painters of the early twentieth century. Barbara Hepworth stood at the edge of a cliff with her eyes closed, arms spread to the wind, drinking the salty air, and Peter Lanyon lay facedown inhaling the rugged Cornish soil (I tried this on the Great Lawn in Central Park, but the police made me leave). My hero Glenn Gould conducted in the air while standing before the ocean and sang Gustav Mahler *lieder* to cows, while Albert Pinkham Ryder took long walks along the Battery of Manhattan to study the moon.

My paintings present the landscape in the same way I learned to see it, by lying on my belly with my chin in the dirt, foreground so close I can taste it and background far away. No middle ground. Seeing from a bug's-eye view instantly compresses space, like closing an accordion, and makes the viewer complicit in reconstructing the landscape; I provide the close-up and the far away, and the viewer supplies the middle. This is nothing new. The Canadian Group of Seven painters from the 1920s and 1930s eliminated middle ground in order to give the spectator the impression of being in direct proximity with the raw power of nature.

Imagine any landscape painting and you'll see a fixed view of a place, which automatically implies someone standing there gazing at that location. The painting acts as a stand-in for the solitary viewer experiencing the landscape. I am obsessed with fixed views and study paintings by Thomas Eakins and George Caleb Bingham because their conceptual rigor is compressed into carefully crafted views. Their paintings are not depictions of motion but subtly articulated affirmations of place. No past, no future, no story. There's no such thing as narrative painting because we don't know what the painting looked like before, nor can we anticipate what it will look like in the future; it is eternally immediate. Why force painting to do what literature, film, and theater do better? We are not storytellers but image-makers. Images begin and end motionless.

Peach Man

Anyone who grew up in 1970s Myrtle Beach will remember the Peach Man, a sunburnt farmer with a crew cut who sat on a wooden crate in front of Chapin & Co., our local grocery store, selling the sweetest peaches in the known universe. Townsfolk also referred to him as Wart Man because of his dubious ability to cure warts with the touch of his fingers. A skeptic, my mother wanted to see for herself and had me hold out my hand. He mashed his thumb against a colony of warts in my palm, and a week later they vanished.

"Are these peaches local?" she asked.

"No ma'am, they're from a mile away."

Thus began my love for regionalism. American Scene painters from the twenties through the fifties were guided by what the anthropologist Clifford Geertz referred to as "local knowledge" and based much of their philosophy on the belief that "To know a city is to know its streets." Painting is local knowledge; it is the evidence of its creation, eternally in the present tense. The Peach Man's awareness of orientation was so resolute that any place beyond the crate under his denim-clad butt was foreign. I am still trying to paint as well as he sat.

That experience also taught me about the ways in which we ascertain truth; two people see the same thing from different vantage points. Art bundles two truths simultaneously, one visible and one invisible. In his sculpture *Dove*, William Edmondson used direct observation and drawing skills to render the appearance of a bird. However, his genius was in breaking down visible appearance to reveal a deeper truth that relies less on visual accuracy than on personal and cultural experience; the second truth can only appear when the first one vanishes, when one thing slips into another. The beauty of a work of art is that it has no real purpose other than to slip, dilating our eyes in the process.

Position

Growing up in a resort meant working in the hospitality business. Every teenager should do restaurant work because it embodies most of the skills they'll need in adult life, such as collaboration, presentation, and how to swallow food without anyone knowing. Plus, you get to say "griddle" a lot. I started busing tables in a restaurant called Slug's Rib at thirteen and was instructed to say that I was the manager's son when asked my age by shocked tourists. The first girl I kissed worked there. She was sixteen. One busy summer night we snuck out of the kitchen and stood on the bank of a river that flowed behind the restaurant. She yanked me by the ears toward her face and commanded me to "open my mouth."

I worked in a different restaurant every summer. By nineteen, I was a kitchen assistant in a Japanese restaurant called Nakato, where part of my job involved taking the trash to the Dumpster at the end of that evening's service. At eleven o'clock, while the last tables were enjoying coffee and butterscotch sheet cake, I'd push a leaking garbage can full of rotting tuna across the gravel parking lot into the thick Carolina night. The dead weight forced me to rest every few feet, when I would utter to myself, "Here I am." The world was spinning, and things were happening everywhere, but the density of the trash heightened my awareness of being in that place at that moment and, like my mother's floating camellias, filled me with a rage to live.

Painting is the same. You make a few adjustments, and here you are. Other people look at it, and here they are. I still think of my paintings as bins full of warm, rotting tuna that I must push from one place to another so I can get home and go to bed; it sure makes them a hell of a lot less precious.

A landscape painter must be aware of the viewers' positions both physically (where they stand) and conceptually (how they will mentally project themselves into the spatial arrangements). Are the viewers included in the composition, or do they bring themselves to it? For example, a landscape by Philips de Koninck and a ceiling fresco by Sebastiano Ricci imply the footprint of the viewer in their compositions; we see the world from a fixed vantage point determined by the artist. Ad Reinhardt's black paintings and Frank Stella's protractors do the same thing, but use the tactile certainty of materials instead of pictorial illusion to mark our physical location in the room. The painting becomes a proxy *for* our eyes as opposed to an experience *to* which we bring them. Looking at a painting is active.

We project our vitality into its world and, like a holo-gram, that world should be complete regardless of our changing position.

Pollock's Studio

On a sticky August afternoon, Katie and I took some friends to visit Jackson Pollock and Lee Krasner's studio in Springs, Long Island. The house and grounds were unremarkable, but Pollock's freestanding studio was arresting. All gazes were focused on the floor with its lassos of drips, but I barely looked down, for this was not an altar for genuflection but a place to work. I was looking for outlets, checking ventilation, imagining where the refrigerator would go, and wondering if you could get Indian delivered. Every studio I've ever been to has drips and splatters, and this was one more on that long list. I abhor the term "drip painting"—people pay too much attention to Pollock's technique, how he painted as opposed to why; I don't think of Lucio Fontana as a hole puncher or Fred Tomaselli as a pill pusher. Pollock let process lead him until technique vanished for an overall experience that washes over us. Focusing on drips is missing the extraordinary power of those paintings. We know that Pollock looked at aboriginal art, Tibetan painting, and the fluid webs of Janet Sobel, who was painting with sticks and drips in Paris in 1945. Mark Tobey was making all-over paintings before 1946, and perhaps Pollock saw those too, but where he took it is more important than where he got it. Pollock worked his later canvases on the floor, which took them from the Western tradition of easel painting into realms of Tibetan sand painting and ritualistic dance, allowing him to be in the image.

Whether brush, knife, squeegee, or broom, a tool is simply an extension of the body and intellect of the artist. Paint is not only the delivery system for ideas, but the flesh and blood of them, as William Carlos Williams wrote, "No Ideas but in Things." That said, Pollock's control of materials was stunning, and any Bozo who says, "I could do that" is full of clown shit. They couldn't, and, more important, they didn't. I want to unroll eleven feet of unprimed duck on the cold floor, give them a gallon of black enamel and a stick, and say, "OK, dazzle me."

Not just anyone can be an artist; it takes intent, execution, rejection, failure, Tylenol, and endless practice. That's before you can even think about showing in galleries. You must also possess extraordinary empathy, circumspection, resilience, and the sense of humor that comes from living an insensible life. Then, it all must be woven into a cohesive, visually compelling body of work followed by another, and another. Not so easy. The comedian Steve Martin said, "It's easy to be great. It's hard to be good."

Moreover, an artist must have a working relationship with solitude. When I was seventeen, I stayed alone in my bedroom doing what every horny teenage guy does: making classical drawings. I drew until my wrist hurt, switching from my right hand to my left, sometimes using both. I drew on every surface I could, even squeezing out multiples until I couldn't produce anymore. Although gifted and talented, I still couldn't call myself an artist. I had to live life to have something to say.

Pablo Picasso was an exception. The breadth and pathos of his early Blue Period paintings, like *The Tragedy* (1903), reveal a sophistication and empathy rarely seen in a twenty-year-old. I have looked at a lot of painting and keep coming back to his staggering genius. *Genius* is one of the most overused words in our language. Someone who scores high on an IQ test or can recall data with the accuracy and speed of a computer is not a genius but simply has proficiency with numbers, an aptitude for testing, and terrific potential. However, genius is measured by achievement, not potential. Don't promise us; show us. Picasso was a genius, but he also worked harder than a choirboy in a porn shop.

An artist is a person who lives in the triangle which remains after the angle which we may call common sense has been removed from this four-cornered world.

—*Natsume Soseki*

Front Room.
Back Room.

I love being fooled. Whether a carnival huckster, con artist, pickpocket, or infomercial salesperson, anyone who hides behind the armor of a carefully rehearsed routine fascinates me. My obsession with infomercials started as a child, and Ronco was my favorite; any problem in the world melted away when the Pocket Fisherman commercial came on. That voice, part carny talker and part uncle, was Ronco founder Ron Popeil. I applied my tip money toward buying the Pocket Fisherman and other miracle inventions like the food dehydrator, Inside-the-Shell Scrambler, and GLH-9 Hair in a Can, which I used in a painting. I wonder who owns that hair-piece. I even wrote fan letters to Mr. Popeil and received cordial replies.

When I type the word *Ronco* on my MacBook, spell-check changes it to *rococo*, and I grin from ear to ear. Infomercials skillfully manufacture desire, which is itself a form of tension, a one-sided longing for that which is craved. If you look beyond the chocolate sipping and ass pinching, you'll find that eighteenth-century French Rococo painting is full of such tension. François Boucher, Jean-Honoré Fragonard, Jean-Antoine Watteau, and Nicolas Lancret painted desperate, lustful pictures, using frivolity to mask melancholy as if something cherished were coming to an end. Rococo images are often dismissed as trivial, pastel-hued, and decorative, three things I happen to love. They are also highly skilled paintings by successful artists. With brushstrokes that glow as if painted with liquefied silver, a Fragonard embodies the conceptual framework of its message, one of fragrant luxury, classical reference, loss, and sexual fantasy.

Some critics and instructors use the word *decorative* pejoratively, as if severity and discord make a painting good. They probably couldn't make a successful decorative painting if their powdered pink cheeks depended on it. What they fail to recognize is that the will to decorate doesn't only arise out of levity and frivolity, but also out of doubt and uncertainty. Reality is questioned, reexamined, and improved through the process of ornamentation. I believe that it's impossible for an artist not to reflect his or her times; however, art is not a mirror, it's a container. Everything goes in, but only the artist decides what to reveal, and how; the painter Robert Motherwell said, "It's an intellectual decision to paint emotionally." Painting should be more than eye candy, but every painter should know how to make really good candy. Studying decorative arts can help an artist integrate disparate elements into a cohesive whole that delights the eyes. Pleasure is, itself, content. Every painting is decorative.

Manufactured desire is equally as enticing as fabricated environments. Every few weeks for the past fifteen years, my close friend the photographer Arne Svenson and I meet for lunch at the Olive Garden in Chelsea; we call it our "Ladies Luncheon" because our spouses are professionals with day jobs. With some of the finest restaurants on earth within a one-mile radius, we go to Olive Garden because it has the kind of watered-down, one-size-fits-all environment that is an ideal forum for our very real conversations. We talk about the art world, share career triumphs, and have supported each other through the deaths of parents all over bowls of overcooked spaghetti and meatballs. I love scripted, corporate hospitality and planned environments because they make those tender, unexpected human moments all the more poignant.

As I type this, I am sitting in a cobalt-blue neon banquette under a fake rainforest at the Peppermill Resort Spa Casino in Reno, NV. Casinos relax me because they are the most honest places on earth; everyone knows that the house always wins. No lies. Casinos are also planned corporate environments that appear to run effortlessly while thousands of workers labor in concealed hallways, offices, and stations operating the controls. Any experience that puts a wide gap between what you pay to see and what is hidden attracts me.

This division between front room and back room is why I don't like restaurants with open kitchens. When I go out for dinner with my wife or friends, I want to be immersed in a carefully orchestrated front-room experience, not see pots of boiling potatoes; I've worked in enough restaurants. Although I labor for months in my studio, my exhibitions are strictly front-room experiences. No one is allowed into the kitchen. My videos are styled after cooking shows for this reason: to give people a glimpse of the boiling potatoes.

Gambling is manufactured emotion.

—*Jack Binion, casino mogul*

Art History

The only thing that truly belongs to a painter is the history of painting. I study art history for one reason: permission. Knowledge can make you formidable, but knowledge paired with permission makes you twelve feet tall and bulletproof. Learning about painters who came before me, both trained and self-taught, Western and Eastern, is not only my responsibility but also pure joy. Painting isn't a nebulous, anything-goes activity but a cumulative practice that requires discipline and scholarship. The notion of the artist as a lightning rod receiving visions from tree trunks is hooey, though there are exceptions like William Blake or Martín Ramírez. The rest of us go to our studios every day, lock the door, and make stuff.

I live in New York City because I am curious about everything, and I want to get there by subway; a MetroCard is a passport to the universe in its totality. New York is also one of the world's great walking cities. My favorite walk is from our apartment on the Upper

West Side through Central Park to the Metropolitan Museum of Art on Fifth Avenue. The Met is the reason I moved to New York City; I am sitting in the Greek and Roman galleries as I type this.

My idea of a perfect Friday night is a late-afternoon walk across the park to the museum with Katie. We enter through the street-level door, unknown to most, and head to the cafeteria for early dinner, a glass of wine, a slice of pie, and coffee. Then we roam the halls until they kick us out. As we move from gallery to gallery, the paintings light up like lanterns, begging our eyes to sop up everything they have to offer. I proposed to Katie in front of Albert Bierstadt's *The Rocky Mountains, Lander's Peak* (1863) in the American Wing. As we gazed at the painting, I compared her attributes to colors (the clear blue of her laugh, her dark chocolate eyes, her pale rose lips) and said if I could fit those colors into a single tube of paint it would look like this. From my pocket, I produced an actual paint tube, uncrimped the end, and dumped a diamond ring into my palm as I dropped to one knee. The security guard gave me a thumbs-up. I chose the Bierstadt because it will hang forever. I want my children, grandchildren, and great-grandchildren to be able to stand in the same spot that we did and feel us beside them, our histories bound in a fixed view. The universe might be totally unknowable, but one thing is certain: painters will walk to the Met.

In a Hurry? Take Lombard

Art is the intensification of slowness. There is rich poetry in antispeed. I love bad Internet connections, tollbooths, and long lines because they are forced interruptions in the blur of getting from one obligation to another. One of the things I miss about old-fashioned record players is flipping the album from side A to B, because that mechanical interruption gave me a full second for the music to ring in my ears while I anticipated what was to come. Many novelists write in longhand on yellow ledgers for the same reason, because it offers a built-in clumsiness.

Painting is a collection of organized interruptions: fractured planes, broken colors, and shifting lines. Real awareness doesn't come in long dial tones of looking, but in the moments of clarity when the eye is halted and restarted, noticing things it may have missed before. My two favorite streets in America are Lombard Street in San Francisco and Chalmers Street in Charleston because they represent antispeed; whenever I'm in a hurry, I say, "Let's take Lombard." In college, when stuck on a painting, I'd drive my car to Chalmers Street, the oldest remaining cobblestone street in Charleston, and drive from one end to the other, one bump at a time. In this rapid, streamlined world, I took solace in knowing that speed wasn't an option.

Art allows us to think slowly because it is made slowly, which is why copying others leads nowhere fast. My paintings are frequently imitated, and you can see many examples on the Internet. Painters have always borrowed from each other—I certainly lifted motifs and color ideas, but I have massaged them into my own visual language over tens of thousands of hours of labor. Give your work time. It doesn't matter where you got it, only where you take it. Be clumsy. Con artists take shortcuts; real painters take Lombard.

Do you skate or are you just wearing those shoes?
—*Tim Kerr*

The Third Thing

My love affair with Ireland was minted in poetry. For as long as I can remember, the works of John Hewitt, Seamus Heaney, Thomas Kinsella, Derek Mahon, and W.B. Yeats have held a secret place in my imagination, and, after winning a Fulbright Scholarship in 1997, I chose to live and paint in Dublin for a year. In addition to Fulbright funds, the Irish Museum of Modern Art granted me a spacious, skylit studio in what was the seventeenth-century Royal Hospital Kilmainham. I kept an apartment in the Rathmines section of Dublin but slept on a cot in that studio most nights. Once a week, I put a drawing pad and toothbrush in my backpack and boarded the next train at Heuston Station with a one-way ticket. My intention was simple; as soon as a place looked interesting, I got off and walked.

Ireland is a country best seen on foot, and it rewards those who are willing to smell and touch every detail on wayward lanes braided with damp hedges beneath downy skies. Walking in Ireland taught me how to break down the landscape into composite parts and relate those parts to the human body. For instance, the foreground is visceral and immediate, my sneakers on wet grass. Middle ground is farther away; I could easily walk there but first must visualize being there in my mind. Background is too far away to walk, so I can only project myself there in my imagination. Three layers of spatial information are compressed into a single view. The greater the distance, the more it is internalized, because I have to imagine being there while standing here.

A landscape painting should relate to the body parts of the solitary viewer, with the bottom corresponding to the feet, a midsection, and a top that refers to the space around the head. My paintings arise in the same way we experience the actual landscape, through a collision of personal experience and empirical observation. Art happens when the intellectual and the visceral collide so violently that they fuse into a third thing. Ireland impressed upon me that there is no room for the landscape in a landscape painting; it must be ripped out to make space for the third thing. Only the viewer can turn it back into nature. A landscape painting is complete when the landscape vanishes.

TOWERING

Tyzack

In 1987, my senior year of college, the world-renowned environmental artists Christo and Jean-Claude flew down from New York City to Charleston for an award ceremony and lecture. My professor, advisor, mentor, and friend, the British painter Michael Tyzack, knew Christo personally and asked me to drive him to the airport to collect them. Their visit was a big, hairy deal, as Christo and Jean-Claude were just coming off the success of their Pont Neuf piece in which they wrapped the loveliest bridge in Paris in sand-colored polyamide fabric, a piece that was seen by over three million visitors.

As Christo and Jean-Claude walked off the plane, I was struck by how delicate they were. After a warm greeting, we walked to Michael's station wagon, and my years of bellhopping in hotels paid off as I efficiently loaded their bags and chauffeured them downtown for a Lowcountry lunch of barbecue (mustard base), chicken bog, buttery biscuits, and sweet tea at our favorite joint on King Street. Christo and Jean-Claude were so kind. I was a tall, goofy twenty-year-old nobody sitting face-to-face with two international art stars, yet they spoke to me with respect, made eye contact, asked questions about my work, and listened to my responses. They even gave me their private number to call when in New York. After lunch, I ran to my studio and painted all night long. I couldn't wait to meet more visiting artists.

Later that year, a midcareer painter who Michael also knew and who had appeared in a recent Whitney Biennial, flew to Charleston from New York for another lecture and exhibition. Once again, Michael chose me to drive him to the airport. This time was different. He welcomed our visitor and introduced me as his finest student. She responded by shoving her luggage in my face. She was arrogant and spoke to me like I was a small animal in a petting zoo. She was clearly part of that tribe of crabby, dreamless urbanites who think that all Southerners just crawled out of a storm drain. Later I went to Michael and confessed my disappointment, a combination of shallowness and anger. I felt like a phony. He winked and said he was teaching me a valuable lesson that I'd have to figure out on my own.

Twenty years later in 2007, as he lay dying of cancer in his James Island home, Michael's wife, Ann, held the phone to his ear so I could say a tearful good-bye to my friend. Michael could hear me, but couldn't speak. I talked about our days together at the College of Charleston, how I felt that anything was possible because he had my back. I remembered how, when the fine arts building closed at ten o'clock, he gave me the keys; when I wanted to work on several paintings at once, he got me a private studio; when people complained that I was hanging my paintings in public spaces without permission, he dealt with them; when I needed a car to transport work, he lent me his station wagon. I never heard the word *no* come out of Michael's mouth, and it made all the difference.

I told him that he was my other father and that I'd finally figured out what he was teaching me all those years ago. Michael didn't bring me along to have me help with the luggage but to show me how a professional artist treats a nobody. Christo and Jean-Claude had nothing to gain by showing me kindness and respect. They did it because that's what pros do. The best artists are also the nicest.

Take care in how you address fellow painters, regardless of their age or résumé. To this day, I answer every email I receive, make time to speak to artists who approach me, see their shows when I can, and treat every single one with dignity, because painting deserves our best selves. Working in the arts in New York City for thirty years has enabled me to meet a lot of famous, successful people, and they have one thing in common: good manners. They are consummate professionals with nothing to prove outside of their craft because everything goes into it. Nothing is left over. The dicks are the ones who have something to prove outside of their work, and I've met plenty.

To them, I say, Thank you for showing me how not to behave. Some people make me feel older and wiser, while others just make me feel older. I don't care if you are having a lousy day—you are still representing your work, so put a cork in it and act polite.

If you ever visit the College of Charleston campus, you will see three paintings prominently hung in the entrance to the School of the Arts: William Halsey on the left, Michael Tyzack on the right, and me in between.

Family Tree

It's fascinating what you can learn with Google, a cappuccino, and thirty minutes. Here are my teachers' teachers. I am not fit to eat off their buckled shoes, but it's still neat to see how all roads lead to Uncle François.

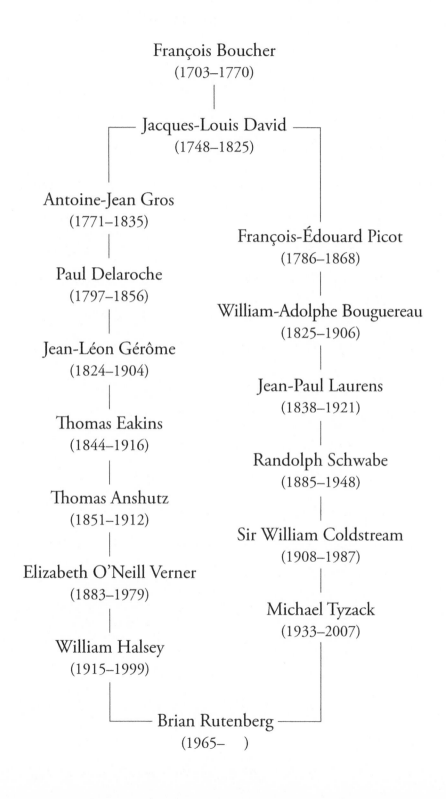

François Boucher
(1703–1770)

Jacques-Louis David
(1748–1825)

Antoine-Jean Gros
(1771–1835)

François-Édouard Picot
(1786–1868)

Paul Delaroche
(1797–1856)

William-Adolphe Bouguereau
(1825–1906)

Jean-Léon Gérôme
(1824–1904)

Jean-Paul Laurens
(1838–1921)

Thomas Eakins
(1844–1916)

Randolph Schwabe
(1885–1948)

Thomas Anshutz
(1851–1912)

Sir William Coldstream
(1908–1987)

Elizabeth O'Neill Verner
(1883–1979)

Michael Tyzack
(1933–2007)

William Halsey
(1915–1999)

Brian Rutenberg
(1965–   )

My Hero

My obsession with the Canadian pianist and philosopher Glenn Gould began on June 9, 1986, during my junior year of college. I know the date because I wrote it on the back of a drawing that I still have. Late one afternoon, Gould's 1981 recording of J.S. Bach's *Goldberg Variations* came on WSCI, the local public radio station. (He also recorded it in 1955, but I prefer the later version for its X-ray clarity and slower tempo.) I set my brush down, sat on the windowsill overlooking George Street, and listened to the entire piece. Gould's performance had an almost Dixieland buoyancy as well as astounding transparency; you could even hear him humming in the background. I was bewitched.

I went straight to the library the following morning to read everything I could about this fascinating creature. There was no iTunes back then, so obtaining recordings was nearly impossible. The college's music library had one copy of J.S. Bach's *Toccatas*, but it was scratched, so my friends drove me to North Charleston to the Paragon, the only independent record store in the area, so I could comb through their vast selection of used records and bootlegs in the hopes that something of Gould's might appear. The Paragon was run by an emaciated albino named Bobby, who looked like a naked mole rat. Rumor had it that Bobby would trade rare albums with college dudes if they masturbated for him in the back room; a guy in my dorm was said to have gotten his Ramones outtakes with the "five-finger discount."

Once I'd devoured every book on Gould, I had to get as close as possible to standing in his shoes. After a 1994 opening of my work at a gallery in Detroit, I rented a car and drove alone to Toronto, where Gould was born, lived his entire life, and died. I sat contently in the lobby of his apartment building on St. Clair Avenue West (he had apartment 902) watching neighbors come and go, ate "scrambles" washed down with Sanka in his favorite booth at Fran's Restaurant across the street, and spent hours drawing trees by his modest headstone in Mt. Pleasant Cemetery. I still keep a laminated leaf from his grave over the doorway to my studio. At night, I'd drive up and down Yonge Street with Gregorian chants blaring on the stereo and the heat turned up to max, because that's what Gould did.

My research also took me to other parts of Ontario. In the town of Orillia, ninety miles north of Toronto, I ate chop suey at Shangri-La Gardens, Gould's favorite Chinese restaurant, which played his recordings on the jukebox at an assaulting volume, and walked down a private road to his family cottage in Uptergrove on Lake Simcoe, where he escaped the world and practiced. Yeah, I was stalking a dead guy. From there, I drove through mighty Algonquin Forest to Ottawa and met with the director of the music division of the National Library of Canada, who gave me access to Gould's entire recorded and written archives. As I was neither a historian, a musicologist, nor a writer, the staff didn't know what to make of me. Why did a weirdo painter from New York City need to see Gould's prescriptions and hold his shoes? I had no idea what I was looking for, yet I'd recognize it on impact. I was desperate to see what an artist's life looked like.

The musician and scholar John Roberts, Gould's oldest friend, happened to be doing research in the library that week and took an interest in my studies. We talked for hours over coffee and met for dinner whenever our paths crossed in Ottawa; it was the closest I would come to having Glenn Gould sitting across the table from me.

My work got the attention of the Canadian Broadcasting Corporation, and they interviewed me on television and radio. In 1999, the Glenn Gould Foundation commissioned me to create a series of paintings to be exhibited during the Glenn Gould Gathering, a symposium of musicians, historians, and enthusiasts from all over the world. I hung out with Ray Roberts, Margaret Pacsu, and Lorne Tulk, all prominent figures in Gould's life. I even sat down at

CD 318, his beloved Steinway, with his piano tuner Verne Edquist, who, like me, has synesthesia. Verne sees color in sound, while I see color in words.

Glenn Gould famously said, "The purpose of art is the gradual, lifelong construction of a state of wonder and serenity." The patience and commitment embodied in that statement continue to inform every part of my life and career. Gould valued solitude as the prerequisite to the creative act and wrote copiously about the role of the artist in society. He believed that the ideal audience-to-artist ratio was zero to one and viewed technology not only as protection from the wildness of nature, but from ourselves, for behind that protective layer every individual would be free to construct his or her divinity.

For Gould, technology and its role in the dissemination of art was not just a philosophy but a moral calling, so he retired from live performance in 1964 to devote his remaining years to studio recordings, sound documentaries, and essays that explored what he called creative lying. He even postulated home kits that would allow listeners to custom design their ideal classical recording by combining various performances according to individual tastes, moving the spectator from passive receptor to active participant in shaping the art form. He was exploring relational aesthetics and personalized music channels decades before Pandora and Spotify were invented. Gould despised live performance for its "non-take-twoness" and spent countless hours crafting his recordings, splice by splice, until they got as close to perfection as possible. He treated the recording booth like a painter's studio in which the artist worked in cloistered solitude, releasing only what was ready for public consumption.

Glenn Gould has been referred to as eccentric, difficult, and even insane. I disagree. He practiced constantly, had a trenchant wit, and didn't take himself too seriously. He gave his life unconditionally to his work and protected that life from outside intrusion. Sounds like sanity to me. Gould also possessed a keen marketing sense and branded himself long before artists were expected to do so. Like R. Crumb, who drew on place mats in French restaurants, he perfected the state of being social and detached simultaneously, eating alone in diners and living anonymously in a ground-floor suite at the Four Seasons Inn on the Park in a Toronto suburb. Gould suffered the stroke that eventually killed him in that room. After his death, it was converted (appropriately) into a storage unit for audio-visual equipment. I snuck in late one night and slept on the cold floor until the sun came up.

Although world-famous for the brittle clarity of his playing and controversial ideas (he wanted to "ban applause" and "try prison"), Gould was also a tender man yearning for transcendence through the poetry of place. Geography was primary to his thinking, especially the vast abstraction of the Canadian north. This deep awareness of internal and external orientation struck a chord in me; his sound documentary *The Idea of North* is still one of my favorite recordings and is best experienced under the covers, naked, through expensive headphones.

Glenn Herbert Gould died a few days after his fiftieth birthday on October 4, 1982, when I was a junior in high school. I never met him and wouldn't have wanted to, because everything was in the work. On the eve of my fiftieth birthday in September 2015, I thought about what it meant to outlive my hero. What is a hero? What do they provide? Heroes don't need us to imitate them. That's easy. They slam the door in our faces so that we have to sneak around the back and pick the lock, only to discover that it's been changed. They say, "Don't do as I do. Figure it out for yourself." Gradually finding one's voice through trial and error is far richer than emulating someone else's. The best teachers aren't those who solve problems, but those who give us permission to create them. My hero taught me how to craft a life as an artist and, more important, how to protect it. It has been said that every work of art is about the loss and regaining of identity. Glenn Gould introduced me to myself.

The Wind

Will Barnet was a great American artist and a gentleman. I met Will through the sculptor John Raimondi, who had introduced him to my paintings. Over many years and dozens of braised pork chops in the dining room of the National Arts Club, where he lived in an elegant apartment upstairs with his lovely wife, Elena, Will regaled us with stories about having Mark Rothko as a pupil, riding the train to Philadelphia with Stuart Davis to teach at the Pennsylvania Academy of Fine Arts, and drinking with Pollock and de Kooning. He even knew Ashcan painters.

Will was fifty-five years older, but he spoke to me as an equal. He loved my paintings and saw every show I had in New York, even when he was in a wheelchair, always leaving a handwritten note. I saw Will for the last time having supper in the club two weeks before he passed away. I knelt down, as he was hard of hearing, and kissed his cheek. He looked at me and said how much he believed in what I was doing, and that I was a real painter. On November 13, 2012, Will passed away at 101. He didn't die—painters don't die. They stand in the wind growing thinner and thinner until only the wind remains. He once told me that the last thing he did before going to sleep was drink a tall glass of ice water. Now I do the same thing. Then I lie down and surrender to the shameless wind.

Greg and Johnny

Two men shaped my early career: the painter Gregory Amenoff and sculptor/dealer John Raimondi. Greg hired me as his studio assistant, supported my work, and got me a gallery job when I was desperate for income. In that same gallery, I met my future wife and had my New York solo debut. His family became mine at a time when I was homesick for South Carolina. Greg also introduced me to one of my best friends, who has championed my work for over twenty-five years, John Raimondi. If Greg is the Empire State Building, then Johnny is the Chrysler Building, each one of a kind. Johnny owns more of my work than anyone else and has placed my paintings in major public and private collections. He has the best eye I've ever encountered and an encyclopedic knowledge of twentieth-century art, and he showed me how to navigate the art world. Greg and Johnny are the big brothers I never had. Both men have been at my side for every important event in my life and career. Most of us are lucky if we get one skyscraper in a lifetime. I got two.

SEEING

Counting Sand

You can't look anywhere in Manhattan without seeing scaffolding stuck to buildings like barnacles on a ship's hull. Every New Yorker has had to cross the street to avoid those steel poles holding up wooden planks—or worse, descend into damp tunnels that run below a worksite and dump people out into another time and dimension like a wormhole in deep space. I love scaffolding because I'm fascinated by the idea of building something to build something.

My childhood goal was to count every grain of sand on earth, as if an inventory of each particle would uncover some greater truth. I told everyone of my plan, even stealing cups, tweezers, and a magnifying glass from my brother's bug-collecting kit. Although less than a thimbleful was actually counted, something far more miraculous happened. I began thinking like an artist. Artists are people who have the right dreams at the wrong time. They set out impossible tasks for themselves and always fall short. For me, it wasn't the number of grains counted, but the guileless notion that it was worth trying in the first place. Sometimes the truth isn't discovered, but manufactured. I orchestrated a consummate failure, gave up, and found lucidity.

Art fails us. It is lifeless and incomplete. We project our vitality into it, and, in return, it compensates us for life's impermanence. By magnifying its limitations, art shows us that perfection is unattainable; it's the longing that matters. All artists live in the gap between what they imagine and produce; no finished painting ever looks as good as the one I see in my mind, but the next one might. Albert Einstein said, "Insanity is doing the same thing over and over again and expecting different results." Art is part skill and part insanity; too much concept or technique comes across as dry and pretentious, while too much craziness without the chops to deliver it in tenable form is . . . well . . . crazy. Shout your nutty ideas to the world; we need more crazy. Society doesn't expect artists to play it safe. Insulate your foolish self from sensible people. If you're lucky, that insulation will last a lifetime, and you'll produce meaningful work, but first you have to make something to make something. Is the real work of art the building or the scaffolding?

Tell me, which is mightier: polished granite or the lucent wings of a butterfly?

Dare to wear the foolish clown face.

—*Frank Sinatra*

Declaration of Independence

Memory is a word often used when speaking about painting, especially abstraction; the artist "paints from memory" or their work is "about memory." I don't believe that painting can be about memory because we don't know what the painting looked like before, nor . can we anticipate what it will look like later. Painting is experience, not the recreation of it.

Vintage photography can document what East End prostitutes looked like, but a Camden Town painting by Walter Sickert allows you to feel their moist breath on the back of your neck because you are inches away from the evidence of its creation. Intimacy isn't represented but innate, because you are standing in the same spot as Sickert when he applied each greasy shingle of color.

Memory requires that some past event made an impression upon or seduced the artist. Therefore, working from memory implies the recreation of seduction, which is the definition of kitsch.

As the product of a beach resort, I admit my first reality was kitsch, and I adore it. Garishness, absurdity, and new things made to appear old fascinate me; placing style over substance suggests a desperate, hasty type of love that is both humorous and melancholic. Kitsch embodies respect for misplaced priorities that I find genuinely beautiful. You will never hear me use words like *corny* or *sentimental*, and I don't like people who do. I hate cynicism in art. Say what you mean from your heart. Duke Ellington said, "If it sounds good, it is good." The same applies to a visual experience. If it looks good, it is good. Authenticity is elastic. I will fully commit to anything that delivers a complex and enduring experience no matter if it was carved from ivory five centuries ago or mass-produced and covered with LED lights last week.

Professor/Philosopher Denis Dutton wrote about "nominal authenticity," which refers to a work of art having been created by its purported creator (not a forgery), and "expressive authenticity," in which a work of art is a genuine expression of an individual's or a culture's beliefs or morals. Knowing one's origins, geographically and culturally, ensures authenticity, but lusting to be something you weren't born into is equally genuine, because you chose it—it didn't choose you. Whatever makes you feel the most like yourself is authentic.

For the first fifteen years of my life, a large framed reproduction of Emanuel Leutze's masterpiece *Washington Crossing the Delaware* (1851) hung over my childhood bed. I spent hours staring at it as my eyes adjusted to the darkness and as the sun filled my room like a tidal pool in the morning. Although I had no idea what the image meant, I sensed the artist transmitting pulsations through the glacial monumentality of the shapes, the solid triangular composition, and the use of red to tug my eye across the center of the image. I grew into a young man under that reproduction, and, one winter's night, everything became clear. Although the picture represents a seminal event in American history, its real power and import lie in the enactment of place—not George Washington's, but mine. That reproduction was not a recreation of a past event, but an image carefully constructed by a skilled artist to intensify the present; it was a declaration of location, not in the musty halls of history, but right there under my sneakers. Emanuel Leutze loved me enough to have made this thing for me to see.

Years later, I begged my parents to take me to the Metropolitan Museum of Art in New York to see the original, and it reduced me to a jellyfish on the floor. Speechless, I stood inches away from the brushstrokes and felt as if it had been painted for my eyes only. Leutze and I joined nervous systems and made something from nothing. We crafted a place and discovered it at the same time.

Look, I made a hat
Where there never was a hat.

—*Stephen Sondheim*

Blankness

I hate snow. For a Southerner, the word should always be followed by "cone" or "globe." My idea of hell is being cold, wet, and having to carry shit. But every couple of years, we spend Christmas with family in Alaska in some of the most rugged and beautiful landscapes I've ever seen. On one such trip, while my wife and children were curled up by the fire, I zipped into a coat the size of a tree trunk and wandered alone into a nearby meadow at dusk. The bruised light made it difficult to see where the mountains ended and the sky began. Every sensation was multiplied. I could hear ice pellets crackling on my shoulders and feel warm blood spurting up my neck with each hiccup of my heart. There was no focal point, only gradations of light. I was standing in total blankness, seeing myself seeing.

Good painting is a container for blankness. I don't mean that there is no content or imagery, but that the painting becomes an open-ended container into which viewers project themselves. Technique vanishes, style fades, opacity gives way to transparency, and, for a moment, you don't recognize what you see. I know a painting is trying too hard when I can describe it.

Art is a form of containment, yet it's important to remember that a container not only keeps stuff inside but also protects it from the outside. Piet Mondrian wrote about the discord arising from the fact that, as human beings, we are neither part of nature, nor able to exist without it. Art ameliorates this tension by allowing us to do things that we can't in real life. When artifice acts as a stand-in for nature, we are free to have an experience for the sheer sake of experience, without the desire for gain or the risk of peril. An actor applying fake blood and collapsing onstage isn't glorifying death but celebrating health, because he or she isn't really injured. Art celebrates life by cheating death. There are so few surprises anymore. Before I leave my apartment in the morning, I already know the weather, the subway schedule, with whom I'll be having break- fast, lunch, and dinner, where the Dow will open, and a summary of world news from the BBC. The farther I am removed from the laws of nature, the more I com- pensate by exaggerating the laws of art.

Speed

Although a painting is a static object, time plays a fundamental role in the viewer's experience. Our attention is like money; we only have so much of it to spend. Therefore, a painter must be aware of the viewer's spending plan. Long, fluid strokes race the eye swiftly from one part of the painting to another, while short, denuded jabs stutter the viewer's gaze, allowing him or her to wander into other areas. Zigzags appear slow, while curves are fast; Picasso often employed these contrasts side by side, especially in the Blue Period. Walter Sickert and Edgar Degas rendered arms and legs in short dashes that ran counter to the length of the limb, slowing our eyes down to revel in fleshy fullness. If I have a particular color combination in which I want the viewer to dwell, I use broken lines and fragmented colors to halt the eye and draw attention to those areas.

I can get a similar effect by using contrasting hues, like bright purple and permanent green or cherry red and cobalt teal, which arrest the viewer's gaze and give him or her time to consider more subtle arrangements nearby. Painting doesn't tell a story, yet it has a beginning, middle, and end. We invest time looking at the surface, dipping in and out of our thoughts, embroidering our vitality onto colored skins, and moving from interior to exterior intuitively. All of this happens in rhythm. Looking at a painting is, at first, like looking out a window on a rainy day: you see either the individual raindrops on the glass or what lies beyond, but not both at the same time. You look at the painted surface or into pictorial illusion. However, a miraculous union rewards the patient viewer. Surface and illusion begin to hum together in a flash of lucidity and expansiveness. Through repeated encounters, the concrete gives way to the transient.

My children ask me when human beings will be able to travel through time; I tell them we already can. We always have. Painting is time travel. A photograph is the same time at the top of the image as at the bottom. However, in painting, it's a different time with every kiss the brush gives the canvas. Hundreds, maybe thousands, of individual moments are stacked like deli meat, all working in unison. You are simultaneously peering back in time and being slingshot into the present. Painting can do what nothing else can: it compresses time and accelerates slowness, as if filming a slug inching across your back porch and then playing the film on fast-forward. My paintings are slugs.

Style

When painting students ask me how to create a style, I tell them that they've just taken a colossal step in the wrong direction. Thinking about style means you are thinking about style and not painting. The best way to find your voice is to make a lot of work and destroy all of it. The most important thing is to show up every day, no matter how dreadful the results. Amateurs worry that their paintings look like they are painted by different people. So what? Try everything and eliminate. A beginner should blend in, not stand out. Stay in the tall grass and work as much as possible. Matisse made a painting, then a painting of the painting. Picasso made paintings of Matisse's paintings. They were fearless, and they worked constantly. It's OK to screw up; just do it gloriously.

I attended graduate school when smart painting—works that required pages of theory, contextual preface, and a short nap—was in high fashion. Classical beauty and emotion were seen as indulgent, seductive, and anti-intellectual. Technique was object driven, and all that mattered were ideas. But viewers shouldn't have to hold a degree in theoretical constructs to look. All they need are two eyeballs and some time. Sure, categories of taste can be refined with experienced looking, but I believe that the mind innately knows when something is harmonious, no degree required.

Museums are full of paintings, but the ones that endure do look better than the rest. Is this good taste or is there some common denominator? Both, probably. It's fashionable to say that beauty can't be defined, or that it's in the eye of the beholder: a claim usually made by those who can't draw or paint. Beauty can, and should, be defined. There has to be some aesthetic paradigm, a set of visual prerequisites. Otherwise, all paintings are beautiful, and therefore none are. George Santayana wrote, "Beauty is the cooperation of pleasures, truth the cooperation of perceptions." Western ideals of beauty are rooted in principles promulgated by the ancient Greeks and Romans, such as proportion, harmony, scale, line, contrast, and the treatment of light. Art history shows us over and over that the thoughtful arrangement of form and the calibration of color can transmit emotions and stir cognition in ways impossible to verbalize. That's why it's visual art.

As a visiting artist, I've given hundreds of critiques in art schools around the world and have seen the problems young painters face when they place ideas before aesthetics. One young man in a prestigious MFA program made six-foot-square photorealistic paintings of his anus in a range of colors (the chartreuse one was kind of pretty). After reading his dense, conceptual statement, I asked him if he had big openings. Bottom line, his paintings were poorly executed and conceptually weak, shock and yawn.

Robert Rauschenberg said it best: "You begin with the possibilities of the material." A painting should grow like a living, breathing thing in which the ideas come out of the process. Starting with an idea and building a picture around it automatically inserts a gap between the artist and viewer because the artist knows something that the viewer doesn't. Even if they figure it out, the gap remains. I want my paintings to begin and end with physical certainties like surface and material; anyone can relate to a buttery brushstroke because it doesn't need to be anything else. Starting with the possibilities of the material allows the viewer and artist to form a social contract on common ground, free to make discoveries together because the painting begins in the artist's imagination and finishes in the viewer's.

Painters like Robert Ryman or Suzan Frecon extract ideas from the limitations of paint itself, developing a way of seeing that is the result of decades of reduction and repetition. A blank white canvas is not a wide-open road but a declaration of limitations, just as every modern piano has eighty-eight keys, yet no two pianists sound alike. The Beatles, Bonnie Raitt, and Judas Priest all began with the same structure: intro/verse/chorus/verse/chorus/bridge/chorus. What makes them great artists is how they flood those restrictions with soul and introspection. Art is the magnification of limitations.

When teachers would say that painting was "whatever I wanted it to be," I felt offended. That's how you speak to a child. Art is not doing anything you want but doing everything you can within walls. Andy Warhol is credited with popularizing Marshall McLuhan's dictum, "Art is anything you can get away with." Don't speak for me, Andy. When I experience a work of art, I want to feel that the artist was committed to more than just getting away with something. Would you want doctors or pilots to get away with stuff? Why would you want artists to? It has taken fifty years, but it finally seems as if the art world is moving beyond the bitter cynicism of Andy Warhol. I am aware of his contribution to twentieth-century culture, but when a real artist like the poet Mary Oliver asks what I plan to do with my one wild and precious life, my answer is more than get away with it.

In graduate school, I worked harder than anyone in the class, and my boyish enthusiasm pissed off an older artist in the program. One night, he emerged from his hate-filled cubby and stormed into my studio drunk, ready to hit me, demanding to know what I cared about and why I smiled all the time. Why wasn't my work cynical? That confrontation was a defining moment in my life because I didn't have an answer, which, in retrospect, was the perfect answer. I was a twenty-two-year-old man-child who only knew how to be himself. Nothing has changed, except that now I'm a fifty-year-old man-child.

Here is a letter to my twenty-two-year-old self:

Dear Brian,

Talent is important, but other factors such as geography, education, health, family, and being in the right place at the right time also contribute to making a career. You work hard, but you had help. Paint from gratitude. Great art can arise from discontent and cynicism, but it can also be born of wonder and serenity. Speak from your heart.

Now dropkick that clown out of your studio.

Yours,
You

The essence of all beautiful art, all great art, is gratitude.

—*Friedrich Nietzsche*

Originality Is a Myth

One of the things Will Barnet and I talked about was the notion of originality. The art world is obsessed with novelty; so many reviews begin with the caveat "Although the artist isn't doing anything new . . ." Painters make paintings, not flat-screen televisions. Our job is not to dazzle critics with the newest model but to act as splicers, fusing personal experience with durable fundamentals from the past. Art students are frightened into thinking that they must be original right out of the gate or risk mediocrity. They face constant pressure to *grow* and *evolve*. Those are art school bullshit words. There is great breadth and poetry in repetition, in doing the same thing for a long time. That's how you get really good at stuff. No one talks about that.

I had three museum retrospectives before I was forty-five, which enabled me to see broad snapshots of my work in clean, well-lit spaces. What I learned was that I only have a couple of moves, but I do them very well. Fortunately, my compositional range, palette, even the way I see the world have remained relatively singular for forty years. Duke Ellington said, "The wise musicians are those who play what they can master."

Painting should nail your foot to the floor so that you spend your entire life going around in a tiny circle. At the center of that circle is one question: Are you making art, or are you manufacturing a state of lucidity and trying to keep it around for as long as possible? If you're focused on making *art*, it will end up looking like someone else's. Your true job is to construct a clear seeing place. Be narrow-minded. You can't manufacture originality, but you can limit your perspectives. Myopia is bad for politics and education, but it's good for art. Galleries are full of paintings that are too damn smart, too global and aware. I don't want the entire globe in a painting; I can get that from the *New York Times*. I want one person's creepy world compressed down to the size of a diamond and shot at my face violently. That will give me lucidity.

An artist should never be the smartest person in the room. I never am. I'm not advocating making dumb, uninformed paintings; I am promoting flying your freak flag on high and letting us stare at you. Give up trying to be new, because as soon as you finish a painting, it's a thing of the past. Forget originality because everything has been done. Give up trying to become rich and famous, because it won't happen. Art doesn't only show us what we can do but what we can't. I continually take inventory of things that will never happen:

I will never be a travel agent or a Pakistani. I will never win the Turner Prize or have a one-man show at the Museum of Modern Art. I give up on stuff that won't happen to make room for what is certain: I will show up every day, lock the door, bend the world through the prism of my experience, and put it back out. Originality is for amateurs; consistency is for artists. Don't ask, "Is it good?" but rather, "Does it continue?" Nail your foot to the floor. Then tell us about it.

There is nothing new under the sun.

—Ecclesiastes 1:9

How Do You Know When It's Finished?

This question is offensive. Who cares? A baker is finished when there's a cupcake. I'm a professional, and I know my job. While some people were busy studying law, medicine, or investment banking, I was learning how to draw and mix color. The reason a lot of modern and contemporary painting appears unfinished is because it is—it requires the consciousness of the viewer to be complete. Painting is like driving a car: your mind wanders, but you still have to operate the steering wheel and pedals. Having painted for forty years, I no longer think while working, yet I'm always in full control. That's why flight hours really count; you can't know when to stop until you recognize what it looks like to go too far. Always go too far and then subtract. There is a fine line separating vital from vapid, and artists must labor through hundreds of paintings to recognize that line. Lorne Michaels, the creator of

Saturday Night Live, said, "We don't go on air because we're ready. We go on because it's 11:30." You can't tinker forever; you have to stop sometime. Experience will tell you when it's 11:29.

One of my best friends is a famous actor. One morning, he and I drove through sheets of October rain from the Upper West Side to Milburn, NJ, to see *Can-Can*, the musical, at the Paper Mill Playhouse while our spouses worked in Manhattan. The show knocked my eyes out. The previous night, I'd seen the comedian Gilbert Gottfried onstage, and his performance summoned the same feeling. There is something about consummate, polished professionalism that brings a work of art to life regardless of the audience.

When I see a lousy painting, a poorly performed play, or a mediocre singer, I feel the unconscious duty to help the artist, tapping my foot to keep rhythm, rearranging colors in my mind, or anticipating a punch line before the comic delivers it. When a work of art is carefully crafted, rehearsed, and repeated to the point of near perfection, it breathes like a living thing. *Can-Can* was a glittery, fire-breathing dragon thumping around onstage, and I was helpless. The same for Gilbert. Great art is always in control.

Samuel and the Urn

I discovered the odes of John Keats in a little bookstore in Florence, Italy, when I was twenty-two and have rarely traveled since without a copy. I've read them on the banks of the Arno, in Irish chapels, at East End Pubs, at NASCAR races, in Las Vegas casinos, and on the New York subway.

My favorite, "Ode on a Grecian Urn," changed the way I think about art and its role in the world. The poem begins with a solitary observer experiencing a work of representational art; the urn is incomplete without the presence of the viewer, just as a painting is lifeless until the spectator projects their vitality into it. The urn is an object that exists separately from ourselves, which produces a fascinating paradox for the figures dancing across its shape, figures simultaneously liberated from time yet stuck in it. They won't age or die, but neither will they inhale the brief fragrance of having lived.

Keats taught me that life isn't a support system for art, but the other way around. Art shows us how to be human. We move through life divided in half, focused on either thoughts or bodily sensations. Rarely are we fully present in both. Art teaches us to be *whole* because it is whole. A painting is two things at the same time: a flat surface with little piles of color and a fictive world into which we expand our consciousness. In a Rembrandt self-portrait, creamy oil paint suddenly becomes translucent flesh with warm blood coursing beneath. Scumbled brushstrokes instantly transform into the folds in a cap. First, there is paint. Then there isn't. Then there is. Every great painter makes paint vanish.

Keats goes on, "Heard melodies are sweet, but those unheard are sweeter." In painting, what gets left out is as important as what stays. Each new brushstroke squeezes out an old one so that a finished painting is half-visible; the other half is the hushed vibration of absence. In his essay *Painting and Time*, John Berger writes, "A visual image, so long as it is not being used as a mask or disguise, is always a comment on an absence . . . . Visual images, based on appearances, always speak of *dis*appearance."

I've been obsessed with the notion of vanishing for as far back as I can remember. I'm not referring to "getting lost in a painting" or "disappearing into the colors," but to the fact that there is a finite inventory of brushstrokes, and, as soon as one is used, it can never be replaced. Does the act of seeing it delete it from existence? Each brushstroke is the last of its kind. Mayflies have a lifespan of thirty minutes; I think of them when I look at the paintings of Albert York. I don't mean that his forms disappear from view but that their brief lifespan in my mind's eye is precisely what brings them to life, so that the next York painting I see is an accumulation of comparisons to the previous one. The best paintings are those you can't describe moments after seeing them. Paul Valéry said it best: "To see is to forget the name of the thing one sees."

One of the great honors of my life was befriending the American poet Samuel Menashe, whose work I discovered in 2005 at the suggestion of the poet William Corbett. I read everything I could get my hands on and then called him on the phone. We spoke cordially and agreed to meet in person. Days later, I was sitting beside Samuel on a bench in Central Park feeding pigeons and talking about life as artists in our great city. He was very interested in my paintings and, over the next six years, came to every show I had in New York. He began to send me handwritten letters that included old poems as well as works in progress and even did a private reading for my painting class at the 92nd Street Y Art Center on the Upper East Side. My students sat transfixed beside their easels in the dark as Samuel stood under a spotlight reciting his best-known works in a mellifluous baritone. For my 2005 solo show at Forum Gallery in New York, we featured one of his poems in the catalog that accompanied the exhibition. Samuel stood at my side during the opening reception and recited Shakespeare from memory for my guests during the lavish after-party at Brasserie 8 1/2 on Fifty-Seventh Street. Here is the poem included in the catalog:

Reeds Rise from Water

rippling under my eyes
bulrushes tuft the shore

at every instant I expect
what is hidden everywhere

Like "Ode on a Grecian Urn," "Reeds Rise from Water" embodies a marriage between nature and art, one hinting at the other. In just a palmful of words, we are catapulted from extreme foreground ("under my eyes") to distant background ("bulrushes tuft the shore") just as a painter uses foreground and background to establish pictorial depth. This technique is an artist's way of declaring love for the viewer, as if to say, "It's safe to go over there. I know because I've already been there for you." A painter should always have the viewer's back, giving him or her the impression that hidden eyes have seen the painting from every possible angle, so that it's warmed up and worn in before the viewer ever arrives.

What astounded me most about Samuel's poetry is how he got such spaciousness into so few words. His work taught me about economy of design, not "Less is more," which I disagree with (Less is less), but clarity of intention. If it doesn't help, take it out. What's the least amount of information your painting can have and be a painting? Samuel is gone now, but I still sit beside him on that park bench in my dreams. We don't speak. The pigeons are enough.

You have to simplify the spectacle in order to make some sense of it. You have, in a way, to draw its plan.

—*Émile Bernard*

WORKING

Drawing

Walter Sickert said, "Drawing is about captivity. Painting is about freedom." The process of rendering the three-dimensional world on a two-dimensional surface is the first step in grafting an image directly onto the nervous system. I have been drawing for as long as I can remember; the thrill of rubbing a No. 5B pencil on cream paper satisfies like nothing else. My favorite thing to draw is a solitary tree, and I've sat under thousands of them, from the jack pines of Algonquin National Forest in Ontario to the sycamores of Central Park and the banyans of Florida, but nothing comes close to the Southern live oak. I am obsessed with drawing their trunks, torqued and full of sad knowledge. Everything I am after in the conceptual framework of my paintings is embodied in that immovable marking of location.

My tree drawings are realistic because my work has to be tethered to the observable landscape; depiction allows for a broader range of expression (political, poetic, formal) because it expands things to which we can all relate. Claiming to represent the act of seeing is provocative, but what does that mean? The reason I draw a tree in great detail is not to make it appear but vanish. Each carefully rendered leaf and strand of bark nudges me further from visible reality into a crafted one, leaving me both depleted and supplied. A good drawing is the visible vibration of its subject. I believe that there is a parallel world running concurrently with this one, and, now and then, we crack into it. Drawing and painting are an attempt to keep that world around a little longer. The coast of South Carolina taught me about the density of place. I am where I go. I love the outdoors but didn't become a landscape painter until I came inside.

Shade, *2002–03, 10×8 inches, pencil on paper.*

Beginning. Middle. End.

Beginning a painting is one of the most exhilarating experiences in the world, a chance to risk everything without being injured or deposed. I start a painting by standing six inches in front of the white canvas, so close that I can see the individual threads and inhale the sweet tang of gesso. Then, with both palms, I make circular patterns, barely skimming the surface with my hands, working from the center outward, feeling every inch of the blank picture plane. The sound of skin against skin and the heat generated from the friction form a binding contract between me and the painting, both physical objects occupying space in the room. This tactile ritual informs every brushstroke that follows. As Sickert advised, "Start like a bricklayer, finish like a jeweler."

Next, I tone the entire surface with an underpainting made of a lean color thinned only with a solvent such as Gamsol—no linseed oil. I observe the fat-over-lean rule: fat means more oil, lean means less oil.

Applying a lean color over fat can cause cracking and shrinking because the top layer dries faster than the bottom. Lean colors such as cadmiums, cerulean blue, and burnt umber are opaque, while fat colors such as alizarin crimson, ultramarine blue, phthalo blue and green, and sap green are transparent. Add more fat as each successive layer dries. Don't analyze when you begin. Turn off the ticker tape. Do first, think second. If it sucks, wipe it off and do it again. Make big shapes, squint, block in masses, and don't edit. Self-awareness is the enemy. Let everything pour out, and then make corrections later.

Painting is delayed gratification; plant seeds now to harvest later. The reason that I begin with a middle tone is to have the option of going lighter or darker. Starting on a white ground means you can only go darker. If I anticipate a warmer final painting, then I'll underpaint in cooler tones like magenta, pale green, or cerulean blue, while a cooler picture gets a warm underpainting of burnt sienna, orange, or cadmium red deep. Gilbert Stuart started with what he called "fog color," a medium-valued gray upon which virtually any color would pop. Sickert used Indian red and pale blue to block in his lights and darks, respectively. Thomas Gainsborough, my favorite painter, used salad tongs to dip sponges into bowls of dark brown to block in generous masses. I love salad and have my own tongs for this purpose.

After my darks are laid in, I paint a series of vertical lines intersected by horizontals, which are quickly smeared away with paper towels; I go through a roll or two every day. The painting doesn't even start until I've wiped away the whole image a few times. My compositions are constructed by placing thick, muscular paint at the bottom with thinner veiled washes at the top to orient my viewer the same way that they experience the real landscape, with the certainty of foreground under their feet and the eye searching the upper distance. Thicker paint at the edges also creates a framing effect, suggesting a picture within a picture, a lurch from one realm to another. Such conventions are nothing new: look at an Asher Durand composition or a landscape by the Swiss painter Alexandre Calame and you will witness the masterful use of pictorial elements (rocks, trees) arranged in a proscenium that frames a view of distant interior space. When composing, I observe the rule of thirds, which divides the canvas into thirds using two vertical lines and two horizontal lines. They intersect in four places, each one a detonation point of energy in the composition.

With the chassis of my image beginning to take form, I inject a sudden blast of intense, saturated color such as ruby red or teal, what a friend of mine calls "letting out the monkey." Doing something crazy and random in the beginning will make you less precious later.

Although I work all day, the majority of my time is spent sitting in a battered rocking chair looking at what I've done. Office workers across the street from my studio have stopped me in front of my building to say they've enjoyed watching me paint, noting how much time I spend backing up and sitting down. Scary, huh? It is important to step back every forty-five seconds to see the entire image. If you don't have a large enough space (I didn't for a long time), then take a picture with your phone. Shrinking the image is a good way to spot compositional flaws; my entire subway ride home from the studio is spent looking at paintings on my iPhone. Most smart phones also have a mono feature, which is good for checking values.

Sometimes all the effort in the world won't fix a dead composition. When that happens, without hesitation, I slice the painting to ribbons with a box cutter, because sometimes a flat line is better than life support.

Day one. Salad tongs and sponges. 2015.

Don't think. Thinking is the enemy of creativity. It's self-conscious, and anything self-conscious is lousy. You can't try to do things. You simply must do things.

—*Ray Bradbury*

Thick Paint

Anyone who has seen my work knows that I pile the
paint on, some areas up to three inches thick. This
technique is called *impasto*. I loathe impasto. Other
than Frank Auerbach, I don't like artists who paint
thickly. I'd rather look at a George Tooker than a
Chaim Soutine. I am not interested in using color in
the service of form but as the form itself. Color and
form are inseparable.

In his book *Art* (1914), Clive Bell wrote, "You cannot conceive a colorless space; neither can you conceive a formless relation of colors." Contrary to my
reviews, I don't use thick paint out of passion, energy,
emotion, or bravura. I use it to establish spatial orientation; thicker is closer and thinner is farther away.
Content is a function of how near or far things appear
from your face.

Some painters work to remove any evidence of their
hand, while others allow the process to be an integral
part of their conceptual framework. Although my

facture is painterly, I've learned a lot by looking at minimalism. As I stand before an Agnes Martin painting, my physical relationship to and awareness of the space around me is amplified because of the deliberate lack of the artist's hand; I become aware of my body standing in the room with an object hanging on the wall. My work thrives on such heightened awareness. I'm a minimalist who doesn't know when to quit. I overemphasize the physicality of my materials to connect the painting to the tactile world that we all occupy. When I throw a fistful of vermillion at the canvas, it splats; if I add thinner, it runs, and one color appears to pass over another because it really does. Think of colors as a pack of playing cards dumped out on a table, a pile of overlapping layers, some visible and others partially concealed. I spend all day stacking color.

I'm obsessed with materials and process, but I don't like technique. This notion sounds ridiculous because anyone who sees my paintings immediately notices the manner in which I apply paint. However, one way to draw attention away from something is to exaggerate it. As the ventriloquist Otto Petersen, of Otto & George, said, "I exaggerate to clarify." Repetition also clarifies. I've always admired arduous, repetitive jobs such as those of traveling salespeople, lounge comedians, or birthday party magicians, who do the same gig three times a day, 360 days a year, perfecting their moves to the point of effortless delivery without a trace of technique. When I washed pots in restaurant kitchens, I took masochistic pleasure in the monotony: dirty pots went in, clean ones came out, and one thing became another through clear intention.

The reason I cultivate a rigorous work ethic and am prolific is to become so fluent with my materials that I can just show up and be with paint. Bob Dylan said, "I want to play guitar without tricks." Picasso spoke of possessing so much technique that it vanished. An artist should never let the audience know how much technique he or she possesses because, if an artist is truly communicating, the content is automatically built into the process; the artist uses precisely enough technique to tell the truth, no more, no less. Practice constantly so you can develop such fine muscle memory that you don't think while you paint. Practice to lose technique instead of acquire it. When the effortless appears difficult, it's entertainment. When the difficult appears effortless, it's art.

H.I.T.

Here is a helpful acronym to keep in mind as you paint: H.I.T.

Hue: Is it warm or cool?

Blues, violets, greens, and raw umber are cool. Reds, yellows, oranges, siennas, and burnt umber are warm. However, such categories are not always intuitive. For instance, cerulean blue is cool because it is closer to green, while ultramarine blue is warm because it has red in it. Alizarin crimson is cool red, cadmium red is warm, and lemon yellow is cooler than cadmium yellow light because it is closer to green. As Hans Hofmann demonstrated, warm colors appear to advance, while cool colors recede.

Intensity: Is it bright or dull?

Think of intensity as a sponge. When the sponge is full of liquid, it is of the highest intensity. Squeezing the sponge drains the intensity. Color straight from the tube is of the highest intensity. Tinting with white will lighten the value but dull the intensity. The trick is being cognizant of value and intensity at the same time.

Tone (or value): Is it light or dark?

Tinting with white or shading with black lightens or darkens the value. Titanium white is the most opaque and brightest white, while zinc white is semitransparent and dries more slowly. Use white sparingly, especially in the beginning, as it can make color chalky and lifeless. Try substituting other opaque lights like flesh pink, Naples yellow, or royal blue for white. Placing the lightest light next to the darkest dark creates a sense of drama and sculpture, while gradations of value feel calm and atmospheric.

A thimbleful of red is redder than a bucketful.
—*Henri Matisse*

Light

Hans Hofmann said, "In nature light creates color; in painting color creates light." I learned to render light by drawing moss-draped live oak trees in the Lowcountry of South Carolina. Everything a painter needs—direct and reflected light, shadow, volume, and line—is bundled under their ancient canopies. Sunlight scatters and drips like glowing, melting desserts when it passes through Spanish moss, and drawing it taught me how to objectify light.

In oil painting, luminosity can be suggested by adding or removing pigment. For instance, begin with washes of transparent color (alizarin crimson, Indian yellow, ultramarine blue, etc.) mixed with Gamsol thinner over white gessoed canvas. After fifteen minutes, remove some of the wash with a clean rag. Wiping into transparent color is a gorgeous way to suggest glow. Conversely, adding layers of saturated opaque color will give a painting the appearance of being lit from within. The thicker the paint, the brighter the color.

To suggest light in painting, you must also recognize
the absence of it. Shade is not the absence of light but
a different kind of light; Claude Monet showed us that
shadows can be full of color and dimension.

Geography plays a fundamental role in an artist's treatment of light and dark. For example, East
Coast light is moist and silvery, hues of cobalt blue,
pewter, and mollusk. Southwest light is bright and
dry, the color of egg yolk and raspberry. Willem de
Kooning's transitions are deliquescent compared to
Karl Benjamin's crispness because they were painted
in different lights. Benjamin lived and worked his
entire career in Claremont, CA, near Los Angeles.
His hard-edged, exquisitely colored compositions are
rinsed in sharp desert light as a reaction to the gestural,
smoke-mirled vernacular of the New York School with
its East Coast humidity. In the Midwest and Great
Lakes regions, American Scene painters such as Dewey
Albinson, Floyd Hopper, Henry Keller, Edna Reindel,
and Charles Burchfield also made significant contribu-
tions to the treatment of light with their broad skies,
long shadows, and crisp lines.

Painters must concern themselves with the laws of
two lights: real and depicted. Is your painting about the
light or the thing being lit? Comparing two contemporaries, such as Winslow Homer and Claude Monet,
reveals two distinct types of pictorial light. Homer's
luminosity is a product of direct observation; he paints
objects that have mass and cast shadows. Form is
revealed through dark and light modeling, symbolic of

the clear morality of a young nation. In France, Monet also began with direct observation but used light not to discover form but obliterate it in favor of a flatter, more democratic picture plane constituted of rapid, staccato brushstrokes.

The treatment of light in nineteenth- and twentieth-century American painting by artists such as Frank Benson, Albert Pinkham Ryder, and Rembrandt Peale was concerned with identifying and rendering the observable world, while the French Impressionists explored light's optical effects, commenting less on *what* we see than on *how* we see. Most painters use light in both ways; witness the work of Giorgio Morandi, whose paintings seem to have light without luminosity. He doesn't rely on light to find form but stacks brushstrokes like strips of masking tape until light becomes form. Morandi isn't painting a picture of things, but constructing a thing standing in for a picture, thus granting us access to something far more provocative: reality.

Compress and Release

Squeeze one end of a water balloon, and the opposite end will bulge. This is a good way to think about pictorial space. Tension can't exist without release. When I apply color, I ask, Is it squeezing or bulging? The water-balloon analogy dovetails with Hans Hofmann's theory of push and pull, in which objects appear to advance when we focus on them, while those in the periphery recede, just as warm colors appear close and cool tones farther away. As I paint, I try to imagine each greasy brushstroke as a three-dimensional object, like a fistful of cake icing. What would the back of the stroke look like? What happens when you stack one on top of another? The viewer sees just the front of a brushstroke on a flat surface, but the painter has to consider all sides, as if standing inside the picture looking out.

The only truth a painter possesses is the flat picture plane; it is the great democratizer, the glorious limitation that joins all of us who dream of light where there is darkness and space where there is flatness. When you observe an artist close one eye and hold out his or her thumb, you are witnessing a violent, destructive act; a Category-5 hurricane, a bull shark attack, and the overthrow of a government all wrapped in a simple gesture that blasts the painter from the three-dimensional world into the two-dimensional plane. The laws of nature are bent to fit the laws of art. Every painting bears the evidence of destructive behavior and violent thought, a breaking down of one thing to expose another. You have to kill something to make something.

Mediums

I spend a great deal of time experimenting with mediums to slow down or speed up drying, and much of my day is spent rotating paintings around the room depending on at what rate I want them to dry. My medium of choice is three parts Galkyd and one part walnut oil. Walnut oil doesn't yellow like poppy and linseed, but, like many nut oils, can go rancid if not refrigerated; it also dries with a brilliant gloss, which keeps colors rich and saturated. Galkyd is a synthetic alkyd resin made by Gamblin Artists Colors that adds viscosity and speeds up drying time. Other siccatives include Japan dryer and copal. I like to mix Galkyd and paint on a palette. Then I let it sit for ten minutes before scraping the semi-dried color up with a knife and applying it directly to the canvas. The resulting color has a sticky, skidding quality that arrests the eye.

When I want to slow drying time further, I add extra walnut oil or put a sheet of plastic over the painting to seal it until the following day. Willem de Kooning laid newspapers across wet paintings as insulation from moving air. Peeling off the paper sometimes left residual texts and photographs, which became secondary images. I love how self-generative de Kooning's paintings are, as if they are part of nature itself, growing and evolving.

If there is a color I need the next morning, rubbers are handy. I drop a big load into a condom, tie the end, and go home. Sometimes I'll saturate a large brush with a dollop of Gamblin's Neo Megilp, no paint at all, and pass it across the wet paint, dragging everything in its gooey path. Neo Megilp, a contemporary version of Maroger medium, is a silky gel medium that maintains body and increases flow. I also use cold wax medium, which is a soft, translucent wax with a peanut-butter-like consistency and which, when mixed into pigment (70 percent paint to 30 percent wax), creates a stiff, matte quality that is useful for making thick layers of color.

Another way to thicken oil paint is to squeeze out blobs onto sheets of newspaper and wait a couple of hours for the paper to absorb the oil and leave dense biscuits of color. Bottom line: the best way to understand mediums is to try everything and not limit yourself to art supply stores. I've mixed oil paint with gasoline, Vaseline, Mazola, pluff mud, Knox unflavored gelatin, salad dressing, dirt, motor oil, blood, and saliva. Yep, it was gross.

Just-spring when the world is mud-lucious…
When the world is puddle-wonderful

—*e.e. cummings*

Glazing

Walter Sickert referred to the question of glazing as "fresh or pickled." I like pickles. A glaze is a thin layer of transparent color suspended in a medium (linseed oil, Galkyd, Liquin, Neo Megilp, etc.) and applied over a dry surface to create a luminous glow, because light hits the paint surface and bounces back to our eyes through the lens of the glaze like a gel on a theatrical light. Alizarin crimson, quinacridone magenta, ultramarine blue, pthalo green/blue, and Indian yellow are excellent for glazing because they are already transparent; however, any color can be made transparent with enough medium. Before glazing, it is best to let the picture dry for at least a week and then, with a wide, pliable brush, apply thin veils, always ending on a vertical stroke to conceal marks.

Glazing with opposites can also dull colors beautifully. For example, a purple wash over yellow paint will bend toward brown. Conversely, applying a transparent glaze in the same hue, such as Indian yellow over cadmium yellow, perylene red over cadmium red deep, pthalo green over permanent green, or French ultramarine blue over cerulean blue, creates saturated blasts of color that leap off the canvas.

Transitions

I keep a bucket of brushes in my studio specifically designated for transitions, the cheap hardware-store variety that are wide and pliant. When blending, I pass the brush over the pigment once and switch to a clean one; if you hit it a second time, you'll kill it. My advice is to kill it. That's how you learn when to stop.

Making convincing transitions in a painting requires being mindful of them in daily life. When I walk New York streets, I pay attention to subtle changes: sidewalks laced with shadows and black blisters of chewed gum, or kneecaps pressed side by side on a crowded subway. As I descend into a station, I close my eyes to heighten other senses, taking in the smell of industrial cleaner and electricity, the clicking of turnstiles, and the warm breath of an approaching train. Every morning, I take the number two express from 72nd Street to Times Square–42nd Street, bypassing 66th Street–Lincoln Center, 59th Street–Columbus Circle, and 50th Street. As we roar past those local stations, I try to read the billboards that adorn the white-tiled walls, but they flicker by in a prismatic blur. I can recognize partial shapes and colors, but not enough to describe them. Painting is partial recognition. Regardless of whether it is representational or abstract, if your viewer can identify and describe everything in your painting, then something's wrong. An eye not told what to see sees more.

I'm often asked if events or transitions in my life influence my paintings. How can they not? Everything makes itself apparent at the appropriate time—not only marquee events, such as births and deaths, but the tender moments that we take for granted, such as watching soap bubbles sliding down a baby's back into milky water, or walking barefoot in the grass on a summer night, or making someone you love laugh really hard. John Lennon said, "Life is what happens when you're busy making other plans." The good stuff occurs in the transitions, and art magnifies them; a painting is a compressed version of an entire lifetime. I'm paraphrasing Johnny Carson, who said, "If you're on television long enough, you'll end up doing every-thing you've ever done." Every painting I make taps into everything I've ever done, all the places I've been, and every person I've met along the way. The longer I paint, the richer the soil.

Breaking Brushes

An artist told me years ago that I treated my work like old shoes, which was offensive to my shoes. My paintings aren't precious artifacts but direct extensions of my studio environment, which is an active, sloppy workspace; I am orderly at home but a filthy pig at work. Except for a few fine sables, I never clean my brushes but plunge them into buckets of warm water and green Palmolive to seal them and keep the bristles soft. When I need one, it is plucked from the soapy water, wiped off with an old T-shirt, and dunked in a bucket of clean paint thinner. Some of my brushes are thirty-five years old; however, when I buy a new one, I immediately snap it in half. Being a brush fetishist reeks of painting as ceremony, conjuring an image of an *artiste* wearing a beret and holding a palette with one eyebrow raised. A precious tool makes precious marks. A broken brush is no longer a magic wand or a conductor's baton but a blunt, compact stub that puts my gigantic hand close to the battlefield. Painting is messy. My tools are clumsy. I disrespect my materials out of respect for my viewer.

Broken brushes. 2016.

The best memory is nothing compared to a good brush.

—*Old Chinese proverb*

Edges

I am always seeking ways to blur the interface between the real world and the painted world. Is the image contained within the edges or does it expand beyond? From 1987 to 1995, my way of dealing with the edge was to eliminate it, so I stuffed my socks and shirts between the canvas and the wooden stretcher bar, rounding the sides of the painting like soft shoulders. I wore only a blue bathrobe for days because all of my clothes were crammed into paintings. Having the image curve around the side and onto the back mimicked peripheral vision because there was no definitive ending. Curving the image also lent the paintings a sculptural presence; some collectors even displayed them freestanding on pedestals.

To further intensify their physicality, I used four-inch-thick stretcher bars and stabbed holes through the canvas with a vicious thirty-year-old ice pick that could take you all the way down to Chinatown. Piercing holes released aggression and forced reality and fiction to collide so fiercely that the threads of the canvas, the stretcher bar, and sometimes even the wall were exposed. Painting is both a lie and a thing; stabbing intensifies both. I don't puncture my canvases any-more, but I still break every brush I own and treat my paintings like old shoes, not for violence but the prom-ise of it.

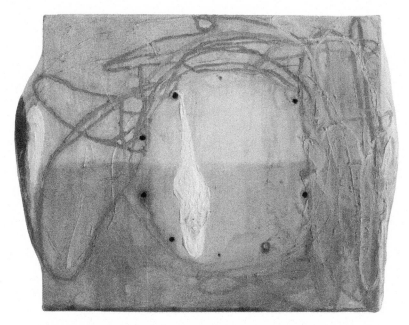

Catawba, *1991, 15 x 20 x 3 inches, oil on linen.*
One of my early stuffed paintings.

To Your Health

Part of our responsibility as painters is making health-ful decisions so that we can devote our entire lives to this thing. I have severe obstructive apnea, a sleep disorder in which the soft tissue in the back of my throat collapses, causing me to stop breathing, a problem that my wife diagnosed when we were still dating. My body has to produce a shock of adrenaline to wake me up to breathe, which puts a strain on my heart, not to mention other lovely side effects like high blood pressure, fatigue, memory loss, and even depression. I was sent to Mount Sinai Hospital for a sleep study and now for the rest of my life I have have to wear a continuous positive airway pressure mask when I sleep. A CPAP is basically a fat person's breathing machine that opens my airway and lets me get the deep, restorative sleep I need to function and paint.

Along with proper sleep, I keep my body limber because painting is a physical activity. Every morning in my studio, I perform a series of stretches developed during my years as a drummer. Here is my routine: remove shoes and socks, sit down in a hard chair, and cross one leg over the other to form a T. Lean forward slowly to stretch the thighs. Repeat with the other leg. Stand up and bow forward, trying not to bend the knees, and slip your hands under your feet, if possible. Hold for one minute. Come back to a standing position. Reach toward the ceiling and wiggle fingers vigorously while keeping shoulders down. Do ten slow windmills with each arm. Sit down and vigorously slap the bottoms of your bare feet. Start painting.

Fresh air is important in any studio, but especially when using solvents and varnishes. I keep my windows open most of the year and use an exhaust fan in winter. Paint rags should be disposed of on a regular basis, and solvent containers should be kept sealed. You should also wear a dust mask when sanding and latex gloves when painting; the gloves can be found at any pharmacy in the bandage and gauze section.

Since I wipe brushes on my clothing, I buy new black T-shirts in bulk; I go through at least three shirts per week. For pants, I wear loose nylon basketball shorts. Since painters are on their feet constantly, attention should also be paid to the lower extremities. My surgeon father-in-law turned me on to compression stockings, which are knee-length, tight-fitting socks that keep my feet from swelling. Comfortable footwear is important too. I wear size fourteen rubber Crocs, which are easy to slip on and off and repel the slop that flies around as I work.

Finally, a bottle of hand moisturizer and a nail file are always on my desk because my mother said that people notice your hands first; decades of nail biting have left me with knobby, Shrek fingers. Fresh drinking water and graham crackers are my snacks of choice, and, in an effort to lose weight, I installed a tropical juice bar in my studio, complete with a blender, bowls of fruit, and a small tiki totem. Every day at noon, I put ice, almond milk, a pint of blackberries, a pint of blueberries, a banana, and walnuts in the blender, and that is my lunch. Although I am grossly over-served at steakhouses, my diet is fairly healthful because the best way to deal with your critics is to outlive them.

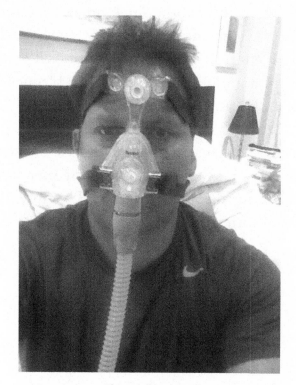

Sleep tight. 2016.

Playing

All painters are connected through their materials. Regardless of ideology, political orientation, subject matter, or geography, we all apply skins of color to a flat surface with old tools. I'm not a Luddite. I embrace technology but also recognize how low-tech my job is: there are no algorithms or data mining. Clearing my cookies means eating a sleeve of Oreos, and storage and retrieval is wiping an image away and repainting it.

There is nothing more ancient and intimate than making a mark with your hand to show another human being. It says, "Hey, I love you, and I made this for you to see." Mark making instantly connects the mind to the hand, and the more complex the mind, the greater the need for the simplicity of play. Italian Renaissance drawings may appear academic and precise. However, they were highly playful. As paper production expanded in the fifteenth century, artists were encouraged to draw with greater frequency, which fostered investigation without preciousness. Drawings were not exclusively preparations for paintings but ends in themselves. For example, Fra Bartolomeo posed small wooden dolls to render the figures in his studies for paintings; Perugino cut, pasted, and gridded his drawings to transfer them into larger compositions. Painters used a process called "pouncing" in which tiny holes were scored along the lines of a drawing with a stylus, which was then patted with black or white chalk dust in a muslin bag. The dust penetrated the holes and left a faint tracing of the original image on the support (panel, plaster wall, etc.) when the paper was removed.

I am fascinated by the tools of work, especially those designed for a specific purpose, inventions so streamlined that they can't be used for anything else, like shoehorns, ice cream scoops, or the food carts that flight attendants roll down the aisles. I bought a used cart to have in my studio because it was the perfect height for my palettes and had plenty of secret compartments for candy. For a painter, everything is a tool for work. Seasoned artists don't only buy their supplies from art stores, but also from bakery supply shops, auto stores, pet stores, medical-supply dealers, sex shops, and hardware stores. If you can hold it, you can paint with it.

Painters also modify existing tools for their specific needs. Jackson Pollock used the nonbristle end of a brush as a dripping stick, Brice Marden extends his brushes with long dowels and applies ink with tree branches, Janine Antoni paints with her hair; Kazuo Shiraga used his feet; and Jules Olitski used squeegees and brooms to push pigment around. My painting table is a buffet of unconventional materials for applying paint, such as the round side of lightbulbs, cardboard boxes, old credit cards, a shovel, women's wigs, shoes, even the flat side of a fish tank because it was the right size. All that matters is the truth of the mark. An artist's job is to monkey with stuff. We don't seek solutions, but problems. We play because we can.

I have been painting for many weeks—Sea, Fish, and the morning redness. Someday perhaps one paper will miraculously bloom before my eyes . . . much must transpire within myself first . . . for painting is no longer painting, but is increasingly the concentrated moments of fleeting clarity. These moments must be sustained and permeate my whole being, for I find that one must be what he seeks to utter—for inevitably one utters what he is.

—Morris Graves

Titles

My titles come from reading poetry. I choose words that don't influence the viewer but broaden their experience, such as *Buckle* or *Clover*. My titles may also refer to a dominant tonality, such as *Silver Favorites* and *Hemlock Lake*, or reflect my Southern origins as in *Saltwater* and *Camellia*.

Many painters claim that a title limits the viewer and undermines the purity of the image. I disagree. The viewer needs limits, and no image is pure. *Untitled* suggests that the painting can be about anything, which is too democratic. Art is not a democracy but a dictatorship. A painter must take a clear, personal stance without telling the viewer *what* to see, only *how* to see it. Painting is open ended as long as the painter keeps one foot on the viewer's throat at all times.

Along with titles, a painter should sign and date their work to signal that it's finished and ready for exhibition. No signature assumes that people, now and in the future, will know the artist. I was taught to sign the back of the canvas because any writing on the front constitutes an image. Unless it is a monochromatic painting, I recommend signing both sides so people can instantly identify your work if they see it again. It will also help future dealers, collectors, and conservators in case authentication is required. On the reverse, I use black charcoal to write my full name, under which I put the title, date, and the initials NYC. Then I spray it with unscented Aqua Net, an inexpensive fixative. Use soft charcoal and don't press too hard; you can see the faint raised imprint of my signature in a large painting of mine hanging in a museum if you know where to look. On the front lower right corner I paint a small BR, which is an homage to the Austrian artist Oscar Kokoshka, who signed his paintings OK. Some painters, such as Albrecht Dürer, Johannes Vermeer, Henri Rousseau, and Maxfield Parrish, intentionally drew attention to their signatures. Arthur Dove usually signed the bottom center and Gustav Courbet painted his name in bright vermillion, which screams, "I am alive. I painted this."

Artists have always been interested in the relationship between language and image, however many contemporary paintings rely on language (descriptions, theories, positions) to exist, often at the expense of intimacy and touch. But language, especially descriptive language, requires a consensus, and the last thing painting needs is a consensus. Every sentence contains a noun and a verb. Changing the order of the words alters the meaning, but it is still a sentence; as George

Carlin said, "You can prick your finger, just don't finger your prick." If I say, "a red wheelbarrow," then you and I form an agreement about the meaning of those words. Language can be translated because it is connected to other known languages, whereas painting is connected only to the painter. Painting differs from language in that it's the physical presentation of its subject, like juggling. A juggler doesn't describe what's happening, because the content is automatically built into the process. All that's required is our full presence in an experience that compresses time and insists we see the world differently for a moment.

Routines

Routines are important to artists because they provide
a layer of protection from the randomness of daily life.
My bedroom closet is full of Levi's button-fly jeans,
a few dozen black Banana Republic T-shirts, a black
belt, black Nike ankle socks, and several pairs of black
shoes. I never have to think about what to wear. My
morning routine is ironclad. I walk my kids to school
at 8:16 a.m. and then hit the gym for twenty-five minutes before meeting my buddies for oatmeal and coffee. Diner culture is alive and well in New York. Every
morning, I see the same people: opera stars, actors,
writers, painters, and travelers. Despite our diverse
backgrounds, we have two things in common: we have
mornings free and seem to be hungry at the same time.

Two of my favorite words in the English language,
besides "sheet cake," are "communal table." I have an
inner ring of close friends and a large outer ring of
acquaintances whom I see on social occasions, but a

diner provides that all-important middle layer—not exactly close friends, but friendly faces.

I get to the studio by ten, stretch, and spend the first hour on paperwork and correspondence. I rarely employ assistants but do everything myself. One of the reasons that I became a painter is because I'm a terrible collaborator; as the adage goes, "A camel is a horse designed by a committee." Lunch is at noon. When a fruit smoothie won't satisfy my hunger, I order food delivered to my studio—usually the same meal for several years until I burn out and never eat it again. I ate so much brick-oven pizza from one joint on Sixth Avenue that they asked if they could put my face on their T-shirts. I never ate there again. My favorite foods to order are Indian and Thai. The delivery guys all know me by name and love to comment on paintings in progress.

My one-thousand-square-foot studio is in a ten-story former printing building in the flower district. It has fifteen-foot-high ceilings and giant north-facing windows under which sits my desk with two computer monitors, a lamp, and piles of paperwork. I prefer consistent light to natural light for painting. I use hundred-watt flood bulbs because I want the pictures to look like they will in a gallery. Music is always playing, and my tastes range from chamber music (Joseph Haydn, Béla Bartók, Gustav Mahler, Luigi Boccherini), 1980s heavy metal (Judas Priest), and jazz (Modern Jazz Quartet, Shirley Horn, and Ben Webster) to the truck-driving songs of artists like Buck Owens or Red

Simpson. I also listen to local talk radio (Brian Lehrer and Leonard Lopate), audiobooks, and a steady diet of podcasts, especially *Penn Jillette's Sunday School, Gilbert Gottfried's Amazing Colossal Podcast, Norm McDonald Live, Here's the Thing* with Alec Baldwin, and Marc Maron's *WTF*. I am also obsessed with archived interviews of Tiny Tim on *The Howard Stern Show* from the 1990s. Those conversations are pure poetry. Herbert Khaury (Tiny Tim) was incapable of lying, painfully polite, and didn't have a cynical bone in his body. He wore no armor and had no filter. I like that.

Regardless of whether it's Bryan Ferry or Terry Gross, sound is just electronic wallpaper that provides a meter that I unconsciously tap into. Having played drums for twenty years, I see and apply color percussively. Painting is rhythm made visible.

Two Common Mistakes

I meet a lot of young and less-experienced painters, and the two most common mistakes they make are not leaving the brushstroke alone and harboring a fear of using thick paint. They put down a mark and monkey with it, killing it dead. Make a brushstroke, leave it alone, clasp your fingers behind your ass, and take five steps backward.

Furthermore, don't be stingy with paint. Better to squeeze out large globs of fewer colors than peck around a palette of too many choices. Mix right on the canvas. Buy cheap student-grade paint if you have to, but use fistfuls of it.

Send my kids to college or buy paint? I bought paint. 2016.

Let It Kill You

The only way to be a painter is to make paintings, and the only way to make paintings is not to do other stuff. With the exception of day jobs, distractions must be kept to a minimum, which means spending inordinate amounts of time alone. Most artists are natural loners, but loneliness is not the same as alienation, which implies melancholy. I was a lonely kid. To encourage more social interaction, my mother made me a fake ID on my sixteenth birthday so I could go out drinking with friends. She meticulously hand-painted a large-scale South Carolina driver's license on cardboard with a square window cut out of the corner. On our back porch, I held the cardboard close to my chest and positioned my smiling face in the window while she photographed it with her Kodak. She printed and laminated the ID, but the first time I tried to use it, the bartender cut it in half. I've never smoked or tried recreational drugs in my life and didn't touch alcohol until age thirty, although I can drink like an Irish poet now. I didn't keep steady girlfriends in high school or college and was still a virgin when my friends were starting families. My friends said I was missing out, and they were right, but being an artist isn't a choice.

The word *passion* is derived from the Latin *passio*, meaning "to suffer." What are you willing to suffer for? I realize that there is actual suffering in this world, and I don't have the temerity to claim to know what that feels like, but are you willing to allow this thief into your room every day to steal your precious time on earth? Painting is a living, breathing thing, and, like all living things, it has to be fed. It demands constant attention and sacrifice; that's why it's called a discipline. Joan Mitchell told me, "Find what you love to do and let it kill you." Life's only commodity is time. How will you spend yours?

When asked if an artist is born or made, my answer is, Both. You have to be born an artist, but that plus $3.00 will buy you a cup of coffee. All the talent in the world is meaningless without an atomic work ethic. An artist is someone who is willing to work harder than anyone in the room at stuff no one else cares about; not many people would spend an entire day mixing pink or drawing a bell pepper until their fingers bled, but I bet you would. Sure, an artist must be born, but what often passes for artistic merit is just an insensible set of priorities. The next time you hear an artist referred to as "critically acclaimed," substitute "colossally lucky and tragically lonely."

I am a great believer in luck, and I find the harder I work the more I have of it.

—*Coleman Cox*

Size Matters

How do our physical bodies relate to our paintings? It is interesting how some artists yield to their size, while others defy it. For example, Frank Stella and Helen Frankenthaler seem too small to produce such massive works, while Joan Mitchell and Richard Diebenkorn had robust carriages that matched the muscularity of their paintings. I'm six feet three inches tall and weigh 245 pounds, which could qualify me as a cast member of Disney World's Country Bear Jamboree. Although the way I move through the world lacks nimbleness and grace, my clumsiness also gives my paintings a power and physicality that matches my stature.

Being tall has other advantages. People can spot me in long lines, I tower above umbrellas on rainy days, and I can breathe fresh air in crowded subway cars while others have to stare at pits and crotches. There are disadvantages too. Theater seats are torture devices, coach class in airplanes is painful, and I have to wiggle butt-first out of taxicabs because there isn't enough space to swing my legs over. Size is a factor in why I became a painter in the first place. I wanted to be a magician, but my hands grew too large to perform convincing sleights. However, my beefy fingers and broad wingspan were ideally suited for wielding fat brushes and fistfuls of color. I'm a failed magician who paints.

Klutz. Jemez Springs, NM. 2015.

Each day I go to my studio full of joy; in the evening when obliged to stop because of darkness I can scarcely wait for the next morning to come. . . . [I]f I cannot give myself to my dear painting I am miserable.

—*William-Adolphe Bouguereau*

SHOWING

Carny

I can paint anytime, anywhere. This is because I made stuff long before I knew what an artist was. I never *aspired* to be an artist; the word makes me cringe because it implies trying to win the approval of others. I started drawing in first grade, painting in fourth, and declared myself an artist at ten. No approval necessary.

My professional career kicked off at eighteen with two sales to a prominent local collector who saw my work in the Guild of South Carolina Artists exhibition at the Gibbes Museum of Art in Charleston. I kissed the check and thought about ways to get my work seen by more people. When you're unknown, the only way to get your work shown is to do it yourself. I exhibited in public libraries, restaurants, corporate hallways, a firehouse, a maximum-security prison, outdoor markets, and medical office lobbies, and even did impromptu shows by hanging paintings on the wrought-iron fences of downtown Charleston. All of those locations had one thing in common: they were places people had to be for other reasons. Whether having pudding or dialysis, people were moving from elevator to escalator, and therefore I had a millisecond to grab their attention.

Other than painting, two of my favorite things in the world are barbecue and magic, both of which can be found at carnivals and state fairs. I always admired the artists who painted circus banners for their design acumen, clarity of intention, and purposeful execution. They taught me that, if you are going to impinge on someone's consciousness, even for a second, you have to grab them by the earlobes with a composition that looks good from twenty-five feet away. By copying such banners, I learned that larger shapes should occupy the perimeter and gradually get smaller as the eye winds into the climax of the image. Carnival posters also taught me that the entire rectangle itself should be considered the first form, just as the four sides supply the first four lines; everything that comes after should relate to those primary truths.

I still paint with the assumption that the viewer has somewhere else to be and I have less than a minute to convince them to slow down and look. From Giotto to John Kensett to Joseph Stella, great painting begins with confident, economical design.

Self-Promotion

Most of my early art education took place in the public library. I especially liked reading essays written by painters that encouraged me to try writing about my work. Along with sales, scholarship is a gallery's job; therefore, the more articulate an artist is, the better the gallery can do its job. Dealers are the conduit between your studio and the public, so a few words directly from you will give them speaking points on which to build; check out the writings of Walter Sickert, Robert Henri, Fairfield Porter, and Gerhard Richter. Writing about your work is as important as drawing and mixing color, because it helps you speak more intelligently in studio visits with dealers and collectors, in gallery talks, and with the press. It's hip to claim that your work will "speak for itself," but it won't. You have to help it.

Before having gallery representation, I promoted myself by reading about how Colonel Tom Parker furthered Elvis Presley's career in the 1950s. For example, I learned how to write a concise press release and design glossy postcards to create an air of excitement about new works. I also invented a fake publicist to send out press packets to galleries and magazines with images and pithy quotes that read well in airplanes, on the toilet, or on airplane toilets. Having a fake publicist allowed me to say, "Let me speak to my manager," which sounded a hell of a lot more impressive than "Golly, sure." An artist must be two people inhabiting one body, a maker and a talker. Artists must brand themselves. This is not a sales strategy, but a way of maintaining focus and, thereby, power. Here are four suggestions that helped me brand myself:

- First, be kind. Many people work hard to create a steady, robust market for my paintings. Being pleasant to work with has gotten me far in this business.

- Second, define your job description. The word *artist* doesn't mean anything. Every pinhead who bakes gourmet cookies is an artist. What is your job? I am not an artist, not a painter, not even a landscape painter, but a Southern landscape painter who lives and works in New York City. That's my superpower under the sun.

- Third, learn how to speak in front of people. Convey to them two things: what you do and how you do it.

- Fourth, send thank-you notes on fine stationery. This practice shows that you took the time to sit down and express gratitude. Not enough people do this anymore, and it makes a great impression.

My self-promotion started to pay off. In 1988, a respected curator from a local college gallery saw my piece in a group show, read about me in a magazine, and asked to visit the studio, aka our back porch. I set up a mini exhibition in our living room. My mother served hot tea, biscuits, and blackberry jam on her wedding china and arranged fists of gardenias in a crystal vase on the table, soaking the air with their scent of thick cream and sugar. Southerners take presentation seriously. I spoke to the curator and his assistant about my process in clear language and, by the second cup of Earl Grey, had landed my first solo show.

In the fall of 1989, my exhibition at Francis Marion College Art Gallery in Florence, SC, opened to the public. I composed an artist statement and printed a price list on which I put a few red dots; the paintings hadn't sold, but the dots created the perception of demand. Four of the paintings did eventually sell, and group shows followed in larger Southern cities like Charlotte, Charleston, and Wilmington.

The next step was mass mailings. I glued small photos of my paintings to sheets of tan card stock and folded them into wallet-sized brochures, which I made cheaply at Kinko's. The front flap featured an image, and inside was a brief statement and list of exhibitions. I'd visit all of the bookstores in the Myrtle Beach area and slide one into every magazine that had to do with art, architecture, finance, travel, local life, food, and design, a practice that continued when I moved to New York. I would visit ten to twenty bookstores in a weekend, even plastering up homemade posters in subway stations. Late one night, at the 23rd Street A, C, E subway station, I saw Keith Haring at the end of the platform drawing on the wall with a fat black marker. We shook hands and continued breaking the law. I don't know if any of it helped, but I loved pounding the pavement and getting the word out.

Here is a basic template for an artist's press release:

FOR IMMEDIATE RELEASE
Title: keep it simple
Who
What
Where
When
Paragraph 1: overview of exhibition (number of works, inspiration)
Paragraph 2: specifics (techniques, art historical references, context)
Paragraph 3: list of exhibitions, collections, awards
Name and phone number of contact. Email address.

(Photo: Wilson Baker)
From a 1993 magazine feature. I was on my knees in Shem Creek, SC, getting attacked by minnows.

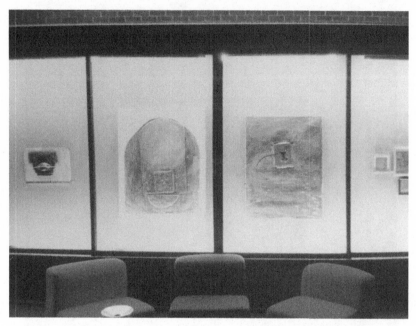

My first solo show. Francis Marion College, Florence, SC. 1989.

Yes, I'll Do It.

In 1995, I had a solo show at St. John's Museum of Art in Wilmington, NC, now called the Cameron Art Museum. The museum paid for me to fly down for the opening and a lecture. I had the flu but boarded my LaGuardia flight anyway, with a fistful of antinausea pills and cold medicine washed down with lime Gatorade. An hour later, I became violently ill. That cocktail prompted a dangerous chemical reaction in which my muscles contracted and froze. Unable to speak or stand, I thought I was having a seizure and that my heart was going to stop. My fingers clenched into sweaty knots, and I gulped down each breath, frothing at the mouth; I couldn't even get my driver's license out of my back pocket so they could ID my corpse. Fortunately, a decisive flight attendant and a wise captain emergency-landed the full USAir Boeing 737 in Norfolk, VA, while two Marines from Parris Island, SC, dragged me off like Keith Richards on strychnine, and put me into an ambulance with full cherry top waiting on the runway. Just as the emergency responders were about to pump my stomach, I threw up and was rushed to the hospital for an examination and intravenous rehydration. An hour later, I felt strong enough to work on some tree drawings in my sketchbook, which piqued the interest of my doctor, who knew a local curator, thus starting a correspondence that lead to another show a few years later. I drove.

Take every opportunity to speak about your work and meet everyone you can; you never know where it will lead. Answer every phone call with, "Yes, I'll do it." When starting out, accept every chance to exhibit no matter where or how remote the location; I've sold paintings to prominent collectors out of group shows in country towns and have had curators contact me after seeing my work in underlit frame shops.

Throughout the 1980s, I drove my blue Honda Accord full of paintings all over the Carolinas doing my fully produced shows, which included paintings, drawings, press releases, a price list, slides for mailings, hanging tools, plastic wrapping, and even a cheese plate for a reception. All someone had to do was say yes, and I'd show up looking like Gomer Pyle on speed and give them a Brian Rutenberg show. When I moved to New York in the late 1980s, I hand-carried paintings one at a time through Manhattan snowstorms and hauled them on jam-packed subways to any place that would exhibit them. Now I have people who say no for me, but, for someone who hates flying, I still do a lot of it.

The pills have been replaced by noise-canceling head-phones and Zinfandel. I thank God when the plane takes off, and I thank Delta when it lands.

Show Business

If you're a painter then you work in show business, and, as the voice actor Billy West said, "There is one show business." Regardless of whether you write string quartets or strip at bachelor parties, you and I have basically the same job. We amplify experience, construct a proscenium around it, and present it back into the world to make people feel alive.

The art world is a multibillion-dollar business, and, like any business, galleries must generate sales to keep their doors open. If they don't think they can sell an artist's work, or if the work doesn't jell with their aesthetic vision, they will pass. This is a business decision. For a gallery/artist relationship to work, each party must have something to gain. The art world is fickle. By the time the newest fashion hits magazines or appears in biennials, it is already outdated. Since many collectors look with their ears, not their eyes, chasing trends is a full-time job and a waste of precious time.

If you want a long career in show business, then become your own best friend, period. The best way to start a career is to keep your expenses modest and expectations low. Ask yourself why you want to paint in the first place. Read *Letters to a Young Poet* by Ranier Maria Rilke and *The Three-Cornered World* by Natsume Soseki, then read them again. They will reveal what an artist's role in the world is.

The artist-to-audience ratio for painting is 1:1. Seeing is a solitary endeavor. Like a hooker, a painting does its job up close, one customer at a time. I find it pretentious when contemporary artists claim to effect social change by hanging their paintings in a gallery. If you want to reach society, use a social medium: start a YouTube channel, write a blog, make videos or podcasts, use Facebook, or make street art. Sitting alone in your creepy studio smearing colors on canvas won't reach the masses, because the masses don't go to galleries. Moreover, claiming to make political art is a marketing strategy; it doesn't mean anything, because *all* art is political. A painting about fracking is freaking great. It's topical subject matter. However, a floral still life by Henri Fantin-Latour or Janet Fish is just as political—more so because it's subversive, masquerading as something else entirely.

Whether you're painting images of chemical warfare or a potful of mums, you're still trying to impinge on the viewer's consciousness and influence the way he or she perceives the world, which is the very definition of politics. Like politicians, artists are part of a constituency that aims to provoke, subvert, and influence others, enforcing the singular message that art knows what's best. A painter uses foreground, middle ground, and background to take the viewer from one place to another just as a politician writes policies to take his or her constituency from this place to a better one.

Even the business of art has political undertones. As I squeeze paint out of a tube, I am reminded that it was someone's job to put it in there, someone with a family to feed and educate, probably without health insurance and likely in an underdeveloped country. With those tubes, I make commodities that are bought and sold in a commercial marketplace because I have a family to feed. I've never been one of those artists who castigates the capitalist art market; I've seen shows in galleries that lambaste the commodification of art, yet there is always a price list at the front desk. My primary representative is Forum Gallery, located at the corner of Fifth Avenue and Fifty-Seventh Street in New York City, the most visible and desirable retail corner on earth. If that's not a political statement, then I don't know what is.

The commercial art market originated in the late sixteenth-century Netherlands. As cities expanded in the thriving trade economy, artists started producing smaller works (landscapes, portraits, and genre paintings) to satisfy a growing middle class. Artists could earn real money selling prints of their paintings, which appealed to broader audiences with modest budgets.

They made work to sell. I receive many emails from artists asking if painting a trompe l'oeil ceiling in their neighbor's kitchen or making watercolors of sailboats because they appeal to summer tourists means they are selling out. Of course they're selling out. So what? Piet Mondrian painted flowers for his entire career because they satisfied a deep need in him, but he also painted them because they sold. Artists have to survive, and that can mean prostituting your skills from time to time. But earning scratch on the side doesn't mean you have to stop making the paintings that fill you with a rage to live, the ones that keep you awake at night. One of my sell-out jobs was designing and building table center-pieces for the International Rock Awards in New York City in 1989. I made a few thousand dollars and hung out with Keith Richards and Ozzy Osbourne. I also gained a story, and, if there is one thing I've learned in my fifty years, it's that you do everything for the stories.

Doing whatever it takes to keep making your work isn't a sign of weakness but of badass, weaponized strength. When I was first starting to hit in major cities like New York and San Francisco in the early nineties, a well-known university invited me to be a visiting artist for three days. The director of the art department said they had come up with a number for my three-day visit, and it was $5,000. I politely declined and told him that it was more than I could afford at the time. He looked at me like the porch lights were on, but no one was home.

"No, we pay you $5,000."

There is nothing wrong with a painter making a lot of money from their work. People who love the romantic notion of the starving artist probably never had to live on Cap'n Crunch or wash their hair in gas station sinks. I always defend painters like LeRoy Neiman and Thomas Kinkade because, regardless of whether or not you like what they do, they are pros who branded themselves and created demand for their works. That's hard to do. Their paintings aren't game changers and won't appear in Art Basel, but who cares? They make charming pictures devoid of discord, but they do it adequately and have a loyal audience. Just because you dislike something doesn't mean you're right. The best way to learn about stuff is by talking to people who love it, because they will automatically know more. When I see a Thomas Kinkade gallery in a mall, I always go in and ask people why they like his work. I hope to learn something. Bottom line, the world is big enough for all of us. The cure for bad painting is more painting.

Working in show business requires an extraordinarily thick skin. People screw up all the time, but you learn to roll with it. Correct spelling is important in a business where image is everything. I have seen my name misspelled in ads, on television, and on museum walls. My paintings have appeared in national magazines upside down and with such horrible color separations that they were unrecognizable. Unless there is time to correct the mistake, I go with it.

Working in galleries in the 1980s showed me the unglamorous underbelly of the art world, and I learned from observation what not to do. I never call or visit a gallery while my show is up. If they need me, they know how to find me. Dealers get annoyed when artists regularly call to ask about sales or to see if any critics stepped through the door. Some artists hang around the gallery and even walk several paces behind visitors as they view the works. Such behavior not only disturbs people but also implies that the dealers don't know their business. Painters should stick to what they know best. Let dealers deal.

Artists have also been known to speak with an air of entitlement. We are entitled to nothing. The arts are a tough, tough business. There are millions of painters out there who would give their bladders to exhibit and possibly sell their work. Any exhibition anywhere is an honor, not a right. Entitlement brings out the worst in people. A man once pulled me aside to ask if I could get his son a New York dealer—at my father's memorial. He'd even brought some of his son's shitty paintings in the trunk of his car. Claude Monet said a painter needs the following things: the ability to work like a locomotive, indifference to everything but the canvas, an iron will, and to not be a cock. OK, I added the last one.

Like most New York artists, I had a bevy of day jobs to support myself while I painted at night. I played in bands and worked in restaurants and hotels and in the storeroom of a posh Italian boutique directly across the

street from Forum Gallery. The bloated Roman manager, Gianfranco, would sit at his desk in a $2,000 silk
suit and flick ashes from his Gitanes onto the white
carpet just to watch me bend over and clean it up. It
was humiliating. Other jobs included freelance illus-
tration, art handling, studio assistant gigs for painters
like Gregory Amenoff and Joseph Santore, and part-
time gallery work. One of the gallery owners, Spencer
Throckmorton, gave me full health insurance for
working two days a week and allowed me to create my
schedule. It made all the difference.

If possible, every painter should do gallery work to
better understand the business side of the arts. The standard artist/gallery split is fifty-fifty. Photography and
framing are generally the artist's responsibility, while
the gallery covers transportation, promotion, archiving,
correspondence, and exhibitions. Dealers receive bundles of solicitations from artists every day, which rarely
lead to anything. However, there are exceptions. Most
connections come through a combination of word of
mouth, a collector's or critic's recommendation, and
sheer persistence. If you feel a gallery shares your aesthetic, then go to their openings and introduce yourself. If you live in another city, then a short letter and
a high-quality color postcard are attractive and professional ways to make an impression. The key word is
professionalism. Use fine paper stock, spell-check, and
splurge for good photography; a grainy shot of a painting leaning against your closet door won't impress a
New York dealer.

Art in America magazine's *Annual Guide to Museums, Galleries, and Artists* is published every August and is a great place to start compiling a mailing list. Websites have become essential, and you can create one for relatively little money. Social media platforms such as YouTube, Facebook, Twitter, Pinterest, and Instagram are the future because they've leveled the playing field. I used to write fan letters to my heroes via agents and publicists; now I can tweet them. Facebook is especially useful: about 30 percent of the people who attend my openings know me exclusively through Facebook, and that percentage is growing.

A real artist/gallery partnership is about loyalty. A dealer sees the big picture and handles business affairs so that the artist can focus on work. They don't make promises but instead say, "Let's start slow and build something." Most of all, good dealers stick with you like family and protect you from outside intrusion so that you can be the most like yourself. I have such dealers.

Every six months, my New York dealers and I meet to go over my exhibition schedule, which is booked four or five years in advance and typically consists of two solo shows with about ten paintings each and a few group shows, commissions, and art fairs. I am represented by seven galleries in different cities, so each one gets a new show every two or three years. Unsold works remain in inventory as many sales happen long after an exhibition. It takes about six months to make a show because I want the paintings to feel as if they were started in one season and finished in another.

Museum exhibitions require a lot more lead time because they consist primarily of borrowed works. They can take up to five years to plan. It is important to keep records of who owns your paintings in case you need to borrow them back. Splurge on professional photography, sign every canvas, and always note the page, year, and issue of every article or review written about you; I had to hire someone to go back through hundreds of articles when my monograph was being produced to get that information.

Most solo shows run for four weeks. Artists claim that certain months are better than others, but I disagree; people will see a strong show no matter what the month, unless it is summer, when most of the New York art world goes to the Hamptons or Hudson, NY. Opening receptions are generally held on the first Thursday of the month. I've had over two hundred of them and still get nervous before each one; it's not how the work will be received that worries me but the thought that people are going out of their way and getting dressed up to come to my show. I worry they won't have a good time.

To get over that, I have rituals. For instance, on the day of a New York opening, I watch cooking shows in bed with hot water bottles under my feet and go out to breakfast with my wife or close friends. Then I eat fried pork dumplings in Chinatown or sit alone in the penguin house at the Central Park Zoo. Most important, I keep a laminated photograph of Neptune, my favorite planet, in my wallet as a reminder of how transient it all is.

My standard opening-night uniform (navy-blue suit and black shirt) is laid out on the bed with five Altoids in the right pants pocket and five Tylenol in the left. Prior to an opening in Boston, I made the mistake of putting Tylenol PM in my pocket and fell asleep mid-sentence at the after-party. Most receptions run from six to eight p.m., but I always arrive fifteen minutes early to personally thank everyone, from the gallery staff to the people serving wine. I slung ice at openings for years, and only one artist (Tony Fitzpatrick) bothered to say thank you.

It's impossible to predict the response to an exhibition or anticipate the turnout for a reception; I've had them jam-packed with a line waiting to get in and others where the entire crowd could fit at a four-top—and did. Three people came to my opening on a frigid night in Detroit in the early 1990s, and I bought them all dinner afterward. Finally, the most important thing to remember is that you can't spend someone else's money. If a piece doesn't sell, it hasn't found the right buyer yet.

To be understood is to prostitute oneself.
                                    —*Fernando Pessoa*

Meetings

Meetings drive show business. Although they require skills that we all learned in kindergarten, such as sitting up straight, making eye contact, and always flushing, you'd be surprised how many people forget the simple stuff. While working in galleries, I witnessed egregious behavior by artists who showed up twenty minutes late dressed like Count Chocula and sat hunched over staring at the ceiling. They shot themselves in the foot because they didn't know how to conduct a conference. Here are some suggestions:

- The most important thing is punctuality. Being late doesn't only show a lack of respect for your time but also for the dealer's. Act like the professional they want to do business with, one who will still be working in thirty years.

- Be easy to work with. A dealer has dozens of careers to manage; you have only one.

- Speak in clear language and without pretense. Avoid artsy-fartsy gobbledygook like, "As momentary replicas become clarified through boundaried and personal praxis, the viewer is left with a clue to the possibilities of our condition." WTF?

- Don't complain. Artists are notorious whiners. If you're having a bad day, then act like it's a good day.

- Dress impeccably. Many young artists try to stand out with radical behavior and appearance, but that takes effort that should go into the work. I discovered long ago that if I projected the appearance of a golf pro, people would leave me alone. Sure, I could dress like Dracula, but being a clean-cut family guy who paints landscapes for a living seems far more radical than wearing a cape. Be your easiest self. My work isn't angry or shocking because I'm not. There are two kinds of angry painters: the mentally ill and those who think that displaying their suffering makes them real. Everyone suffers. We all experience misery, joy, ecstasy, and loss. Put it where it counts: in the work. If you aren't empty when you leave the studio, then something's wrong.

- Smile. You're not selling totes umbrellas.

Totes

Before I had a family, I'd paint for sixteen hours a day and then get dressed up to go out with my dirtball friends; my energy was boundless. These days I don't even put on pants unless it's absolutely necessary. I paint for a few hours, grunt as I sit down, and suddenly wake up with a rope of saliva dangling from my chin. I grunt when I stand up too. Painting is a physical activity. My ankles look like ham hocks at the end of the day and my muscles get sore from lugging heavy canvases around the studio. For relief, regular back and scalp massages are part of my routine. I've been going to the same guy on Hester Street in Chinatown for decades, where I can get an hour-long deep-tissue massage for forty dollars. It's nothing glamorous; I strip down to my boxer briefs, lie on butcher paper, and sleep like a fence post. No talking. I loathe chitchat during a massage.

Years ago, at an expensive resort in Hawaii, a masseur told me that I had a body like a wild boar. I thanked him in hopes of preventing any further ungulate talk, but had to lie there naked for an hour wondering what he meant. My ancestors spawned in the Mediterranean, so I am a hairy guy, but why a wild boar? Ripped muscles? Coarse fur? Poor eyesight? Wet nose? I once made the mistake of telling a masseur that I was an artist, and he pulled out his slides. Not wanting to hurt his feelings, I looked through his entire portfolio on the table and said, "I didn't realize that painting like this was possible." Now I say that I'm a totes salesman.

Weirdo

Painters are creeps, and we've codified a series of cordial questions designed to gauge how well the competition is doing. Here are some examples translated into English. I've heard them all:

"Where do you store your paintings?"
Are you selling?

"Do you build your stretchers?"
Can you afford to have them custom built?

"How do you ship your paintings?"
Do you have a dealer?

"I didn't realize that painting like this was possible."
Kinko's is hiring.

"Do you have any drawings?"
I didn't realize that painting like this was possible.

"I went to your opening last night. You've done it again."
I didn't realize that painting like this was possible.

"I love your work, but I'm not very sophisticated."
I can't control my verbal diarrhea.

"I've never heard of you."
Not only have I heard of you, but I'm so jealous that I could cut myself.

"Let's have coffee."
Fuck you in the neck.

Making It

Young and inexperienced painters talk about "making it," getting their big break. I did too. Here's what I've learned. There are no big breaks, only the gradual accumulation of experiences that nudge a career forward. There is no such thing as making it; there is only the painting you are making right now. I've had hundreds of exhibitions, have stacks of awards, reviews, books, and catalogs, and earn a great living. By every definition of success, I've "made it," but it's never enough, disgusting as that sounds. The secret to longevity as a painter isn't glamorous: Work hard and don't ask for help. Help hurts. When asked how to make it as a writer, Charles Bukowski replied, "Quit now, you suck." If that simple, declarative statement is enough to discourage an artist, he or she should do something else. Waiting for a break is a waste of precious time. Nothing happens unless you do it yourself.

A friend of mine had three paintings in the Whitney Biennial in the late 1980s. He informed me that his life was about to change forever because he'd finally made it. He rode the subway from his apartment in Queens to the black-tie reception on Madison Avenue and took the same subway home. Nothing happened. He sells real estate now.

Love every show no matter where it is, because what goes up always comes down. Careers aren't made in your tux but in your Crocs. If your day job doesn't leave enough time for painting, wake up earlier. If you don't have a big studio, do small work. Seek out experiences. If someone offers you tickets to the opera, take them. If they ask you to help their douche bag friend move boxes in a garage, do it. If there's a lecture on beavers at the museum, go there. See what life looks like. It's takes effort to become expansive.

People often ask me what happens when I feel uninspired. The answer is nothing, because I don't get inspired. Inspiration is unreliable. The only thing I can rely on is a work schedule. When I feel blocked, I keep painting because that's my job. Day after day, I show up and hack away at the gigantic, slow-moving iceberg in my studio. When a piece breaks off, I get a painting. That isn't luck, but stubborn persistence. Working every day puts you in the position for good and bad things to happen. Deciding to leave in a mistake isn't luck, it's practice. When tired, I put my head in my hands and sleep. Then I wake up, eat a peanut butter cup, and get back to work. It has taken me forty years and much more than ten thousand hours to develop the chops necessary to create the illusion that painting is effortless and spontaneous. It is neither.

So little of what could happen does happen.

—*Salvador Dalí*

Rejection

Pain is a great teacher. I mentioned earlier that I keep a pillowcase full of rejection letters in my studio as a reminder of the role that failure played in galvanizing me. If you're afraid of looking like a fool, then please quit now. Society doesn't look to artists for sound, responsible decision making; our job is to strip naked and stand in traffic. Early in my career, I sent out hundreds of envelopes full of slides to galleries, and all of them were returned, some without as much as a form letter. It was depressing, but I kept going; all it takes is one nibble.

A prominent New York dealer left a message on my answering machine in the early 1990s requesting that I come to the gallery in person. Could this be a meeting to talk about representation? I got a haircut, showered, put on a luxurious black turtleneck, and took the R train to Prince Street in the heart of SoHo. I bounded up to the front desk with a toothy grin and introduced myself to the receptionist, a dour little man wearing an even more luxurious black turtleneck. Without making eye contact, he held out my sheet of slides as if it were a used condom. Wait, it gets worse. Affixed to them was a yellow Post-it note that read, "Don't let this guy come near me," signed by the gallery owner. He didn't even have the decency to remove the note. I was humiliated. Ten years later, that same dealer expressed interest in my work, so I did what any self-respecting artist would do: I wrote "Go Fuck Yourself" on a Post-it and sent it to him.

Sometimes humiliation is paired with physical pain. At a meeting with a prestigious midtown dealer, I pulverized a 1929 Ludwig Mies van der Rohe Barcelona chair when I sat down. At 245 pounds, I'm what people refer to as a "chair-breaker" and have crushed many of them at dinner parties, restaurants, and on the beach. There is simply no way to look sexy while fumbling to stand up like a newborn foal, dropping papers all over the floor, and putting a chair back together in stunned silence.

I've made a fool of myself in front of even larger crowds too. My first public slide lecture was a disaster because I planned to "speak from the heart" and instead blanked in front of two hundred people. Each click of the projector was like an ice pick to the scalp. Now I never take the stage without notes. Here are the lessons I learned the hard way: When speaking in public, always have a bottle of water, do a sound check an hour before to familiarize yourself with the equipment, and appoint someone to sit nearby in case of a technical issue. As you speak, skim the foreheads of the audience, but avoid eye contact, because you'll only see the guy getting REM sleep.

Exhibiting your work in galleries also opens you up to professional rejection. Over the years, I've had stacks of reviews—most of them great, some raves, and a few pure suck. Edward Sozanski, chief art critic for the *Philadelphia Inquirer*, disliked my work so much that the dealer wouldn't even let me read the review; she bought all the newspapers within a few blocks of the gallery. She needn't have worried. I never read my reviews—not out of apathy, but because I already possess enough self-doubt that I don't need it articulated by a writer. A few years later, Kenneth Baker, critic for the *San Francisco Chronicle*, gave me a rave review that my dealer said was one of the finest he'd ever read in that paper. I was grateful but didn't read that one either. A good review can be just as disruptive as a bad one because it's natural to want to repeat good behavior.

Art critics have a job to do, and so do I. Mine is to show up every day and make my paintings regardless of whether people like them or not. Worrying about critical reception is harmful because it removes the option of failure. Every painting fails before it succeeds. Mine look gorgeous the first day, but they nosedive quickly, so I spend the next six months trying to get them to hum again. I still get rejected, and it stings for exactly 1.75 days, but I'm a professional. Processing rejection is just another important layer in my tackle box, no different from drawing the human figure or mixing violet and yellow to make brown. Failure is not a lack of ability but a badge of proof that you're working and learning. There are many things to fear in life (viruses, plane crashes, bagel pizza), but there is no upside to a fear of failure.

Be soft. Do not let the world make you hard. Do not let pain make you hate. Do not let the bitterness steal your sweetness. Take pride that even though the rest of the world may disagree, you still believe it to be a beautiful place.

—*Kurt Vonnegut, Jr.*

Feel Your Own Pain

Shortly after moving to New York City, I was in a downtown studio with an older, well-known painter and a few friends. He gathered us in a circle and asked, "Who here is a painter?" My hand shot up instinctively. He peered over his bifocals and said, "OK, you can leave." The room fell silent as I awkwardly made my way to the staircase with a lump in my throat. My brain didn't know whether to make anger or tears. At the bottom stair, I realized something that changed my life; as if I'd turned on windshield wipers in a storm, suddenly everything appeared clear and close. Don't be the first to raise your hand. Don't be so sure. There will always be someone better than you, but there can never be anyone like you. At the bottom of a staircase in a downtown loft in 1988, I gave myself permission to stop trying so hard. When I learned to expect nothing, I got everything.

Art schools teach critical thinking and technique, tools designed for the upside of a career. But what about the shit storms? What about the creative blocks, lack of money, lack of space, bad reviews, no reviews, rejection letters, bad business moves, and general feelings of inadequacy—and that's not even counting the stacks and stacks of lousy paintings that require storage. We must own all of it. An artist is like an onion; peel away the layers, and there is no more onion. Doubt and uncertainty are essential layers in a complete tackle box.

Every painter needs a constituency for pessimism, a person or persons with whom they can be negative away from the pressures of the art-world clown car. Your constituency should be made up exclusively of artists because they're the only ones who understand the day-to-day stuff; nonartists mean well when they offer advice like, "Why don't you just get into the Whitney Biennial?" or "You should get the *New York Times* to review your show." However, they don't understand that an artist needs the entire rotation of life's experiences, good and bad, to tell the truth. Regular jobs demand your peak performance, but only art requires your crappiest, most miserable self too. John Lennon said, "No one can harm you, feel your own pain." Without negativity, you can't be delusional, and self-delusion is what makes art possible, for every creative endeavor begins in a flash of googly-eyed crazy. How could human beings perform delicate brain surgery or write string quartets without first believing that they mattered and are going to live forever?

My early paintings were awful. I never wanted to be great, just less awful. Success is too often confused with popularity; it's gross that a film has to gross $100 million to be successful. Art doesn't work that way. True success is curiosity and effort. Popularity is given and taken away by others, but curiosity and effort are yours alone.

Painting has never been more vital than it is right now, and we are living in it. As I said before, painting is local knowledge; it plants a stick in the mud that says, "We were here," and lays a trail of crumbs so that we may find our way back home again. Although painting can educate, protest, memorialize, confront, and provoke, it cannot change the world; but it can alter one person's world by filling his or her remaining moments of life with supreme quality. If you reach one person, then you've made the earth a better place. Don't be afraid to make bad paintings. Die a little death now and then; you'll be okay. If you make a mistake, scrape it off and start over. No one cares if you screw up. There are no talent scouts. You're on your own. Your work doesn't have to be groundbreaking—it doesn't even have to be good, but it must continue. So lock your door and make your own clear seeing place. It's easier than you think. I've told you how I did it. Now it's your turn to do it better.

Acknowledgments

Thanks to my editors, Richard Koss and Dara Kaye. Thank you also to Rachel Christenson for her superb design, and Courtney Calon, Meghan Harvey, and Girl Friday Productions for their expert guidance and attention to every detail.

Special thanks to:

Robert & Cheryl Fishko
Jerald & Mary Melberg
John Raimondi & Ralph
  Cantin
Gregory Amenoff
Nancy Toomey
Timothy Tew
Nicola Lorenz
Niccolo Brooker
Jillian Casey
Louis Newman

Karen Winer
Kevin Dao
Mary Hurt
Gaybe Johnson
Chris Clamp
Grace Cote
Jules Bekker
Corky Davis
Randall Morris & Shari
  Cavin
Spencer Throckmorton

Paul & Helen Anbinder
Steve & Maddy Anbinder
David Shirey
Chuck Close
Darby Bannard
Ursula Von Rydingsvard
Judy Pfaff
Wolf Kahn
Robert Rauschenberg
Theresa Duran
Phil Freshman
Kathy Schnapper
Ron Porter & Joe Price
Jeff & Jodi Salter
Robert Gilson
The 92nd Street Y Art
    Center
The Fulbright Program
Irish Fulbright
    Association
Robert Gamblin
Steve Bates
Tippy Stern-Brickman &
    Michael Brickman
Joe Santore
Basil Alkazzi
Helen Du Bois
Amr Shaker
Susanna Coffey
Joyce Robinson

Dennis Elliott
David Ebony
John Dorfman
Martica Sawin
John & Kim Rutenberg
Michael & Melissa
    Rutenberg
Jim & Joan Peck
Fritz & Jenny Reinbold
Mark & Colleen Reuland
Valerie Morris
Karen Jones
Arthur McDonald
Mark Sloan
Douglas Ashley
Steve Rosenberg
David Kowal
Barbara Duval
Alan Lokos & Susanna
    Weiss
Russ Gerlach
H. Allen Holmes
Arne Svenson & Charles
    Burkhalter
Virginia Friedman
Jim & Betsy Chaffin
Spring Island Trust
Brookgreen Gardens
Paul Matheney
Jeffrey Day

Tom Starland

Declan McGonagle

The Irish Museum of
   Modern Art

James Quinn

Herbert Khaury

Ernie & Joanne Garcia

About the Author

Widely considered to be one of the finest American painters of his generation, Brian Rutenberg has spent forty years honing a distinctive method of compressing the rich color and form of his native coastal South Carolina into complex landscape paintings that imbue material reality with a deep sense of place. He is a Fulbright Scholar, a New York Foundation for the Arts Fellow, and a Basil Alkazzi USA Award recipient, and he has had over two hundred exhibitions throughout North America. Rutenberg's paintings are in private collections all over the world and are included in such public collections as the Butler Institute of American Art, Yale University Art Gallery, the Bronx Museum of the Arts, Provincetown Art Association and Museum, the Ogden Museum of Southern Art, Peabody Essex Museum of Art, Greenville County Museum of Art, South Carolina State Museum, and many others. He lives and works in New York City with his wife, Kathryn, and their two children.

For more about Brian Rutenberg,
please visit www.brianrutenbergbooks.com
and www.brianrutenbergart.com.

Made in the USA
Coppell, TX
04 September 2022

82617715R00187